Culture Bump: 8 Steps to Common Ground

Dr. Carol Archer and Dr. Stacey Nickson

ISBN: 978-0-578-51233-4

DEDICATION

This work is dedicated to the memory of

James Willie Nickson
and all the ordinary men and women around the world leading extraordinary lives of love and service.

CONTENTS

PREFACE

Culture Bumps: 8 Steps to Common Ground (and what is common ground anyway?)
by Carol Mae Archer

When my co-author, Stacey Nickson, suggested that this personal reflection would be a good way to begin our book, I was both excited and nervous. Excited to tell the truth about this journey and a bit nervous because it is very personal. This journey began for me many years ago—in the cotton fields of West Texas where I first encountered (what I would later call culture bumps). The Aguilar family lived next to our cousin in our small town and in the Fall of the year, when we butchered hogs, I would accompany my father when he carried the severed heads to Mrs. Aguilar and return with him to pick up the packages of amazing pork tamales wrapped in corn husks that she had made for her family and ours. The smell, the taste, the texture was totally different from the mashed potatoes and roast that my mother cooked on Sundays. And their home with the multi-colored serapes draped over sofas, the candles with pictures of saints and the musical sound of Spanish language was so different from our small farmhouse. It was all so different and (probably because the tamales were so good) very intriguing to me.

Years later, when I left the United States for Argentina, I carried that positive expectation that had emerged from Dona Aguilar's amazing tamales with me. However, the reality of living in Argentina was far different, and I discovered I had few or no skills for "navigating the differences." From my encounter with a bidet in Buenas Aires to friends greeting one another with kisses to torrid tangos—I culture bumped everywhere! I returned to the USA and tucked these culture bumps away and if anybody asked me, I lied and said I had no problems in Argentina.

But several years later, when I moved to Algeria in North Africa, the differences were so huge and, in many cases, so difficult to face, that I could no longer ignore them. It made no difference that I *knew* Algerians and Americans have a very different orientation to space—when I went to buy stamps and there was no line, simply a crowd of 30 people—all speaking at once—very loudly—I experienced multiple culture bumps. When I sat in a restaurant and several Algerian young men sat in front of me and looked at me (I was quite interesting to see), Edward Hall's groundbreaking work on proxemics meant little. I simply wanted to (a) hit them or (b) slink under the table. When these incidents were multiplied by the 100s on a daily basis, I was overwhelmed. And upon my return to the USA, when I attempted to sort through my experience, the best advice of "respect differences" and "have an open mind" offered me very little guidance. I sadly concluded that there was something terribly wrong with me because I didn't really know how to respect differences, and I seemed to have no control whatsoever on opening or closing my mind. I finally surrendered to my failure with other cultures.

And it was out of this despair and surrender that the culture bump was born. I had reluctantly decided to leave the field of education—in fact, I was mentally composing my letter of resignation in October of 1978—walking on the University of Houston campus under a gorgeous blue Houston sky, when I had an epiphany.

I suddenly intuitively knew that there was nothing wrong with the Algerians and even more importantly, there was nothing wrong with me—that I had simply had millions of culture bumps.

And the image of two large bubbles gently bouncing off of one another appeared in my mind's eye. Furthermore, I understood that those culture bumps were actually the key to my comprehending—not only the Algerians—but **ESPECIALLY my own cultural being and ultimately my own humanity.** I have spent the last 40 years exploring every facet of that amazing revelation under that blue Houston sky. I have further had the privilege of sharing this exploration with thousands of people from around the globe.

What I have discovered and what I would like to leave with you is my absolute certainty that we human beings can connect with one another authentically and consistently—no matter how different we are—no matter if we agree with one another or not—no matter if we even like one another!

We can still connect as human beings—we can move beyond our differences **WITHOUT** resolving the differences. In fact, this has happened to many people. It happened to me with the Aguilar family, but because I did not understand the process by which it occurred, I could not replicate it in Argentina or Algeria.

My work suggests that there is an observable process by which this happens. And because it is observable it is teachable. We can learn to connect. There are four specific skills that are necessary for connecting:

(1) Managing our emotional response to culture bumps,
(2) Recognizing and articulating our own and another's expectations of behavior,
(3) Defining the meaning for having our expectations met and
(4) Having a conversation with "the other" about those meanings.

Our human connection emerges from that particular type of conversation. And amazingly that conversation cannot happen without our differences.

The differences are the key—the passage to our connection. And that is what this book is all about—your guide to connecting with literally anyone you wish.

For over 40 years, individuals and groups of people have been using the Culture Bump Steps to acquire the specific skills and strategies that are immediately applicable in everyday life and work—in small encounters and in life—changing encounters. The term culture bump was coined by Carol M. Archer and first used in a cross-cultural communication class at the Language and Culture Center (LCC) at the University of Houston in 1978. She defined it as "that phenomenon which occurs when an individual has expectations of a particular behavior within a particular situation and encounters a different behavior when interacting with an individual from another culture."1

She further defined expectations as the expected "normal behavior as learned in one's own culture."2 In other words, it is very simply a cultural difference. The theory which emerged from giving a name to this universal phenomenon clarifies why we human beings sometimes connect with one another and sometimes detach. The theory serves as a solid foundation for the 8 Step Protocol described in this book that leads the practitioner to discover "how we are the same" rather than merely "why we are different."

It is the hope of the authors that in the following nine chapters you will discover treasures in every culture bump that you encounter for the rest of your lifelong journey.

HOW TO USE THIS BOOK

The Culture Bump Steps

1. **Pinpoint the culture bump**
2. **Describe what the other person(s) did**
3. **Describe what you did**
4. **List the emotions you felt when the bump when happened**
5. **Find the universal situation in the culture bump**
6. **Describe what you would do or would expect others to do in that universal situation**
7. **List the qualities you feel that action demonstrates**
8. **Ask or think about how those qualities are demonstrated by other people**

The Culture Bump Steps are the heart of the Culture Bump Approach, and each of the 8 Steps is treated separately in the following eight chapters. Each chapter is designed to make sure that you are able to extract the maximum benefit from each step. There are three parts to each chapter:

1. Introduction
2. Stepping into Action
3. Diving Deeper

The introduction to each step contrasts the way people typically react to encountering a difference with the way Culture Bump encounters differences. In other words, the introduction shows why the Culture Bump Approach is different. The next section, "Stepping into Action," gives precise instructions on exactly how to do each of the 8 Steps. The instructions include tips for and cautions about doing the step. These instructions are useful for either an individual or a group of individuals such as a class or a study group. In addition, groups who have opposing perspectives about politics, religion, ethnicity or other incendiary themes can use the steps to find a common ground from which to begin a dialogue.

Therefore, there are special instructions for these groups who disagree with one another. Finally, "Diving Deeper" gives some background information about the step and suggestions for further study. After the 8 chapters for each of the Steps, there are four appendices:

1. Appendix A has the five Culture Bump stories and an analysis of each story using the Culture Bump Protocol.
2. Appendix B has a more complete theoretical explanation of the Culture Bump Approach.
3. Appendix C presents a historical overview of the development of the Culture Bump Approach
4. Appendix D has three blank Culture Bump Protocol forms that you can use to analyze your own culture bumps.

But, before we begin, let's hear five people tell about actual culture bumps. These stories also demonstrate the four primary categories of culture bumps: (1) the different things we say to one another, (2) the different ways that we communicate with one another, (3) the different ways we behave with one another and (4) the different objects we encounter.

First Story: "I can't believe he said that!!"

My name is Joy from Minnesota, USA, and I had a culture bump with a nice, young man from Venezuela named Miguel. It happened like this. I had just introduced him to a friend of mine, Karen, who was another woman from the USA. She and I were in our forties while he was in his late twenties, but we were all graduate students at a university. She had mentioned that she was divorced and at one point in the conversation, had also mentioned that she was going out with several guys. He said, "So you are an international girlfriend." We all broke up laughing. I had never heard anybody say anything like that before. I could have just ignored his comment and gone on, but then I thought—hey, that caught my attention—maybe it's a culture bump. And when I actually analyzed the incident as a culture bump, I discovered some amazing things about myself and about him and Venezuelans. It was most interesting. You can see my entire analysis in Appendix A and I'll share each of my steps with you as you go through the next eight chapters.

Second Story: "What is that big box and what is it doing on my street?"

My English name is Steven and I come from the People's Republic of China. I came to the USA for 6 months with a group of trainees from my company, the Chinese National Petroleum Company, to have special training at a major university. My group and I had so many culture bumps—from the moment we got off the plane! Things like putting ice in water to drink and tipping in restaurants?? But one of our biggest culture bumps happened the third day we were in the USA. It was a beautiful Saturday morning, a blue CLEAR sky (culture bump) and we three friends, Luo, Eva and I, decided to take a walk and explore our neighborhood a bit. As we came around the corner from our apartment building, we saw what looked like a small house sitting on the corner. As we got closer, we realized it wasn't a house; it didn't have a door but it had writing on it and a large scoop on the front. The word, Donations, was written on the side. We double checked the meaning of the word in our dictionary. Yep! Donations means *Juankuan*. We know this is a box and we know donations means *Juankuan* but none of this makes any sense to us. Luckily, we learned how to analyze our culture bumps in our class. Check us out in Appendix A and we'll share our steps about the big box with you in the following chapters.

Third Story: "What is going on in the house of the Lord today?"

My name is Mike and I live on a farm in Texas. A couple of months ago, my good buddy, Lawrence, invited me to go to his church for a special service on Sunday afternoon. I was looking forward to it. Oh, I am White and Lawrence is Black and I guess that's why this all came about. I got there and everybody was very nice and friendly. I felt very welcomed but maybe a bit underdressed. I noticed that most of the men were in suits and ties. I wish I had known about that. At any rate, during the service, Lawrence, stood up and walked out of the sanctuary. As he did, he raised his right arm up in the air, with his finger pointing straight up. I couldn't believe my eyes. I thought he was mad or something. I just sat there and wondered if I should get up and follow him. But in a little bit, he just came back in and sat down. Only later, did I finally ask him about it and that's when I realized it was a culture bump. I learned a lot about me and about him. You can see my culture bump steps in Appendix A, but I'll dole them out to you one by one as we go through these chapters together.

Fourth Story: "Get on with it already"

My name is Janice and I have a pet peeve with my husband, Don. He interrupts me when I'm talking. It irritates me to death. It doesn't help for me to point it out to him. He just says that I tend to go on too long or sometimes, he even apologizes. But nothing seems to stop him. As I've talked about this to other women, I find a lot of my friends have a similar experience. So, I decided to do the Culture Bump Steps on this. And when I took the time to go through them, I was surprised. You can find out why in Appendix A or just follow along as I share each of my steps with you.

Fifth Story: "Not on my campus you don't!!!"

My name is Carol and I have taught at a university for the past twenty-five years. I've worked with lots of my culture bumps with students and folks from other countries but this was the first time I'd used the idea on something that really upset me in politics. I was reading the Sunday morning paper, drinking my coffee and reading about a guy running for office in my state. There had been a shooting (again!) on a university campus and he had been quoted as saying that we needed more guns on campus. I literally spilled my coffee! I was so upset that I threw the paper on the floor—arguing with nobody in the room. Finally, I thought that maybe I should practice what I preach in this case. To be honest, I wasn't sure if culture bump would work on something like this but I sure was willing to try. You can find out what happened in Appendix A and see each step just as I took it in the following chapters.

Each of these stories show that the practice of the 8 Steps allows us become more competent in all areas of our lives in being able to:

- Manage our emotions
- Identify and describe a bump
- Identify and describe own expectations
- Identify the meaning of our expectations being met

SECTION 1

STEP ONE: PINPOINT THE CULTURE BUMP

The objective of step one is to isolate a reality from a perception of an experience and frame it as a culture bump.

1

PINPOINT THE CULTURE BUMP
(OR NAME IT AND CLAIM IT)

How do we think and talk about those things that catch our attention—things that we find "odd," "different," "rude," or even "aww nice"—things that we do not expect?

Step One is concerned with paying attention to those things that catch our attention. Such things generally register in our mind as thoughts such as "I can't believe he said that," "Look at the way she is dressed," "That's weird," or simply "Whaa?" They can be things like:

- The way a church service is conducted
- The way the clerk at a convenience store acts toward me
- The way a husband talks to his wife
- The way somebody is dressed
- Things that we see on the street

In other words, a culture bump occurs anytime that we find our self in a different, strange or uncomfortable situation when interacting with persons of a different culture.[11] As seen in the list of examples given above, the definition of culture ranges far beyond national culture to include thousands of identity groupings—including different age groups, different ethnicities, different professions, gender differences and much more.

So, in Step One we move from our perception that "this church isn't worshipping right" to "I had a culture bump with the preacher in that church." And in so doing, we take ownership of the experience and shift our paradigm for dealing with a difference.

Paradigm Shift from Macro-Cultural to Micro-Cultural

The first step, pinpoint the culture bump, drives a fundamental paradigm shift in how we attempt to understand one another from a *macro-cultural* focus to a *micro-cultural* focus.[12] In the *macro-cultural* approach which underpins multiculturalism or diversity studies, the focus is on understanding the characteristics of a large group of people who share a set of common values, behaviors and concepts that are acquired through generations. Because this Approach deals with people as a group, it minimizes individuality and views people as products of their culture. However, the Culture Bump *Micro-cultural* approach comes to an understanding of a different culture by looking at one specific act of a specific individual or at a specific object from that culture. So Step One shifts the focus from understanding Them (a group of people) to a personal experience with a specific individual.

Drawbacks of the Macro-Cultural Approach

The *Macro-cultural approach* has been criticized because its' group focus leads to stereotyping and categorizing.[13,14] Shaules argues that individuals and cultural understanding are much more complex and suggests that culture bumps "are a sign of a cultural learning process at deeper levels of self." Abdallah-Pretceille agrees that human beings are infinitely complex and we encounter only fragments of one another's culture. These fragments, however, can be accessed through understanding our culture bumps. So Step One, by pinpointing a "fragment" that we encounter, and then calling it a "culture bump," automatically opens the door to a new paradigm for understanding ourselves and other people.

Advantages and Possibilities of the Micro-Cultural Approach

With the *Micro-Cultural* Approach, we experience ourselves and other people as individuals who have a unique mixture of personal and cultural behaviors that change and develop as we interact in a complex process with multiple cultural groupings. When we pay attention to the individual actions and objects that catch our attention, we can learn about both the uniqueness and the culturality of anyone, anywhere.

The Micro approach is also embedded in the language of Culture Bump. Simply saying the words, "I had a culture bump with_____," subtly shifts us from the feeling of being controlled by someone or something else to feeling that we have choices and a possibility of interacting confidently with people who are different. The language suggests that we are not merely powerless recipients of the behavior or action of a culture bump. Secondly, using the term "Culture Bump" suggests to our brain that the incident may not have been directed at us or at our group intentionally. It casts doubt on whether we really do understand the intentionality of the other person(s)' action. And third, the language suggests that we can experience ourselves as being separate from and more than our culture. Our two cultures bumped, but we and they are more than our respective cultures. They – like we – HAVE culture; neither we nor they ARE culture. Finally, naming the experience as a "culture bump" rather than an intentional personal act reveals the possibility of something beyond culture, something that is more universal. By merely paying attention to an unexpected action or object, we begin to consciously notice our own cultural identity. Simply saying the words, "I had a culture bump" focuses our attention on ourselves and reverses our intuitive response of fixating on what the other person(s) did. This counter-intuitive response results in:

- De-personalizing the incident
- Empowering ourselves to interact confidently with people who are different
- Creating a possible connection with ALL other people at a universal level

So, this Pinpoint step essentially de-personalizes the incident and launches the culture bump user on an analysis of his/her experience. And that analysis shifts differences from being a problem to being a possibility. It opens up the possibility of understanding ourselves as cultural beings in addition to understanding people from other cultures—a possibility of interacting with anyone, anywhere.

This pinpoint step is the key to unlocking the secret of Hall's early insight about the nature of culture and our identity.

> Culture hides much more than it reveals, and strangely enough what it hides, it hides most effectively from its own participants. Years of study have convinced me that the real job is not to understand foreign culture but to understand our own.[15]

Finally, using the term "culture bump" reveals exactly who, what and which action caught our attention and this specific information provides a shared frame of reference for people from different backgrounds to speak precisely to one another. As Archer and Nickson pointed out that when the term culture bump is understood by all parties:

> Learners from disparate backgrounds immediately create a shared frame of reference for conversing about a particular experience. It is at once accessible and non-confrontational

and provides immediate detachment. The term itself impersonalizes the incident and acknowledges two truths: (1) Each of us is more complex than a culture, and (2) each of us is empowered to respond to bumps, even those that are enormously complex, with confidence and authenticity.[16]

The objective of Step One is to separate the actual behavior from our perception of an experience and call it a culture bump.

2

STEPPING INTO ACTION—PINPOINT THE SPECIFIC ACTION THAT SPARKED YOUR PERCEPTION AND CALL IT A CULTURE BUMP

In Step One, you make your own experience of a "difference" conscious and reframe it as a culture bump.

So now you might be asking yourself, exactly how do I "work" Step One? How do I pinpoint my culture bump? It is really simple and brief. There are two simple parts: name the person(s) or thing that caught your attention and then tell what your perception was—in other words what did you think about it. Secondly, reframe how you see it by calling it a Culture Bump.

For example, Joy in the first story says,

> "I had a culture bump with what the Venezuelan guy said to my friend and I thought it was funny."

In the second story, Steven and friends say,

> "We had a culture bump when we saw a donation drop box on the street and we thought it was "weird."

In the third story, Mike says,

> "I had a culture bump when Lawrence left out of a church service in a strange way."

In the fourth story, Janice says,

> "I had a culture bump when I was telling my husband about my day as we were driving along when he just interrupted me to talk about a bird he saw flying along. I thought that was rude and probably happened because I am a woman."

In the case of Carol's culture bump with a politician, she says,

> "I had a culture bump with a politician in my state about carrying guns on university campuses and I thought it was outrageous and stupid."[17]

It's that simple! Even if the same thing has happened repeatedly, it's important to choose one particular incident to use for this step as well as the following seven steps. Now all you have to do is complete the following sentence:

I had a culture bump with____________________and I thought that was____________________.

More suggestions on HOW TO DO STEP ONE
Pinpoint the culture bump

INSTRUCTIONS

1. Recall an incident where you have noticed something different or when you have felt different. One way to do this is to answer the questions:
   - Who did what?
   - Where?
   - When?

2. Ask yourself if it is:
   1) a different object,
   2) a different behavior or action
   3) a different communication style or
   4) a different way to say something.

3. If the bump has been repeated, focus on one particular time—perhaps the first time you encountered the bump or the last time.

CAUTIONS

- **Don't** try to tell a story about this.
- **Don't** forget to use the term "culture bump."

Special instructions for groups with opposing points of view.

Groups from different "camps"—whether they be political parties, religions or age groups—must first agree to use the Culture Bump Steps about a specific incident that one side will experience as a "bump" while the incident is completely acceptable to the other side. *The primary difference between the way groups with disparate opinions actually apply the steps is whether they do the steps with one another or separately. Fundamentally, we need to be conscious of* ***what*** *we say,* ***when*** *we say it and* ***with whom*** *we say it.*

Group analysis of a culture bump

We had a culture bump with________________and we thought it was________________.

Group Analysis for groups with opposing viewpoints

In this step, both sides simply agree that something did occur. For example, someone did say something or a particular action did occur.

Step One should be done all together. This is critically important in order for the two sides to proceed. This is very different from real life in which opposing camps frequently begin their discussion by talking about their very different perceptions or opinions. In this step, however, they begin by jointly identifying something specific that is problematic for one side and acceptable for the other group.

3

DIVING DEEPER INTO STEP ONE

Step One deals with our perception of a particular event. And since our first response to a difference is experienced holistically as a perception, it is helpful to understand more about what a perception is. A perception consists of our thoughts, emotions and understanding. In regard to perceptions, Archer writes:

> Since each person is simultaneously an individual, a member of a family, and a member of a culture at large, no event—even if viewed by twin brothers—would be perceived in exactly the same way. Once individuals are from different cultures, the possibility of completely different perceptions of the same event increases a hundredfold. Let us look for a moment at exactly what happens in the perception of an event.
>
> 1. Language, being a categorizing system, determines how an event is organized. For example, *gordo* in Spanish can be a nickname while its translation in English, fat, is usually an insult when applied to an individual.
> 2. It is primarily our culture that teaches us the criteria we have for determining that which is good, bad, beautiful, ugly, respectful and so on.
> 3. It is again primarily our culture that teaches the various appropriate responses that we have for responding to any situation.
> 4. The fact that we choose one event over another is

culturally determined. Our culture teaches us to distinguish between noise and information, to pay attention to this and to ignore that. When an individual goes into a new culture, there are many things that people in that culture "see" that the newcomer does not. Yet the newcomer will notice things that the people there do not.

5. Sensory responses to events have been shown to be partially...culturally determined. For example, Japanese and Americans have differing abilities to hear certain sounds. [18]

Therefore, if we begin with describing our culture bumps, we have a better chance of understanding our own and other people's differing perceptions.

SECTION 2

STEP TWO: DESCRIBE WHAT THE OTHER PERSON(S) DID

The objective of Step Two is to describe the behavior or object (culture bump) without judgment or interpretation.

4

STEP TWO: DESCRIBE WHAT THE OTHER PERSON(S) DID *(OR JUST THE FACTS, MA'AM)*

While Step One is concerned with paying attention to those things that catch our attention, Step Two (or the Action Step) *is concerned with paying attention to how we describe our culture bumps.* Generally, our descriptions of an incident register as a combination of our feelings and our thoughts such as:

- "She is so rude—Look how she just keeps butting into my conversation"
- "What a bully! He got right in my face"
- "He was really funny—cracking jokes about her"
- "It was just sitting there like a big box in the street"
- "The preacher just stood there like a statue with no passion or fire in him"
- "She set me up and then came at me. She shoulda spoke up"
- "One more of those nut-job politicians who doesn't know squat"

Descriptions Versus Perceptions

In reality, these are not descriptions but are "stories" that we tell ourselves and others to explain the unexpected action or behavior, words or objects that we encounter. They are stories that reinforce and add flesh to our perceptions about an incident. These stories undergird our intuitive perceptions of the situation—perceptions that reflect our life experience and values—most of which are so normal that we don't notice them. Our perceptions genuinely feel like reality. And we rarely pause to understand where our perceptions are coming from. It seems obvious. It is only when our perception is juxtaposed against a differing perception, that we even become aware that we have a perspective. It is our reality. However, when we listen to someone else talk about the same incident we gradually accept that our "reality" is actually our perception. Then, depending on our personality, we either discount their version of the event or discount our own. We assume that somebody is right and somebody is wrong.

Step Two steers us outside of our personal perception to finding an objective description. This movement from a judgmental observation of what occurred to a "true" descriptive observation is fundamental because it shifts the focus from merely acquiring knowledge to "discovering and constructing" knowledge. This is possible because:

> Culture bump theory and methodology emerges from an interpretivist framework of inquiry *(a form of qualitative research)* that assumes reality or realities are constructed by the knower. Culture bump theory thus approaches cultural differences assuming that a hermeneutic conversation *(an exploratory conversation)* between members of different cultures can construct a shared reality.[19]

And a shared reality isn't right or wrong; nor does a shared reality negate any of the other realities.

Why We Think What We Do

A shared reality is only possible if we become conscious of why we believe, feel and think the way that we do. Carspecken dubs these everyday criteria for understanding reality as validity claims. These validity claims are really just the reasons we have for our feelings and ideas. In his Model of Validity Reconstruction, he explains that all human beings presuppose some ideas to be true as we move through life.[20] In other words, we claim that certain ideas are true. Furthermore, he says these validity claims or truths are either—objective, subjective or normative. So, our assumptions about reality are either:

- Objective (meaning everyone everywhere agrees about it—a fact),
- Subjective (meaning it is based on my interpretation rather than a fact)
- Normative (meaning it is based on one group of people's idea of what is a fact)

The examples at the beginning of the chapter, using words such as *rude, butting in, bully, right in, funny, cracking jokes, big, like a statue, shoulda, nut-job* are all subjective or normative. There is virtually no objective description in the list. Carspecken's model can be used to explain both Step Two and Step Three as well as Step Six. Step Two asks us to make objective claims about the culture bump—in other words, to provide an objective description of the incident rather than our perception of the incident.[21] Only by giving an objective description, is the incident accessible to any other individual. And only by giving an objective description, can we begin an authentic and impartial analysis of our culture bump. Therefore, Step Two of the Culture Bump Protocol is a structured way in which individuals experiencing a culture bump delineate their objective claims about the situation—in other words, tell exactly what happened.

So, if the first step, pinpoint the culture bump, is the driver of a micro-cultural approach, the second step is the pivot point to a new road of understanding ourselves and others.

The objective of Step Two is to describe the behavior or object (culture bump) without judgment or interpretation.

5

STEPPING INTO ACTION—DESCRIBE WHAT THE OTHER PERSON(S) DID

In Step Two you describe exactly what you saw, heard, touched, smelled—using only descriptive language.

So now you might be asking yourself, exactly how do I "work" Step Two? How do I describe my culture bump? While it is somewhat artificial, you report exactly what happened with no interpretation. If we examine Step Two in our stories, we can see what this looks like.

In the first story, Joy reports

> "Miguel said, 'So you are an international girlfriend.'"

In the second story, Steven and his friends say,

> "We saw a wooden box (5'X5'x5') with a tin roof and an opening in the front, situated on the street. On one side, it had writing that said, 'Donations of clothing, shoes and toys.'"

In the third story, Mike says,

> "Lawrence stood up and walked out of the sanctuary while raising his right arm up in the air, with his index finger pointing straight up."

In the fourth story, Janice says,

> "I said, '…so then Barb texted me that she couldn't come to lunch because she was too busy. And I felt like that was pretty-' Don said, 'Wow did you see that Mexican eagle fly by over there?!'"

In the case of Carol's culture bump with a politician, she says,

> "He was quoted in the newspaper as saying, 'This guy went in there and was able to kill nine people and injure about a dozen others,' said C.J. Grisham, an open carry activist who is running for state Senate. 'We won't have to worry about such a shooter going completely unchecked until law enforcement can get there 20 minutes later. At least we'll have a chance.'"[22]

Now all you have to do is complete the following question/sentence:

What did the other person(s) do or say? ______________________________

or in the case of an object:

Describe it physically: ____

More suggestions on HOW TO DO STEP TWO
Describe what s/he/they did

INSTRUCTIONS

1. Keep it simple.
2. One way of testing whether or not an observation is judgmental is to ask the question, "Would I know that without being inside the head or heart of the other person(s)?" If the answer is yes, the observation is descriptive; if the answer is no, then the observation is judgmental. Distinguishing between these two types of observations is a skill which is developed in this step.
3. Another way to determine whether your observation is actually descriptive is to ask yourself if your observation could have more than one interpretation. If the answer is yes, then it is probably objectively descriptive. For example, "She is crying" could be interpreted as she is "sad," or she is "nervous," or she has something in her eye or she is "angry." In other words, the objective description could be verified by any other person.

CAUTIONS

- **Don't** try to tell a story about this.
- **Don't** add how you felt or your thoughts about the incident.

Special instructions for groups with opposing points of view.

Groups from different "camps"—whether they be political parties, religions or age groups—must first agree to use the Culture Bump Steps about a specific incident that one side will experience as a "bump" while the incident is completely acceptable to the other side. *The primary difference between the way groups with disparate opinions actually apply the steps is whether they do the steps with one another or separately. Fundamentally, we need to be conscious of* ***what*** *we say,* ***when*** *we say it and* ***with whom*** *we say it.*

Group analysis of culture bumps

What did the other person(s) do or say? ______________________________

or in the case of an object

Describe it physically: ____

NOTE: This step is the same for groups and individuals—except the group members may vary slightly on details.

Group Analysis for groups with opposing viewpoints

In this second step, both sides find a specific example of what they disagree about. For example, liberal minded folks in the USA might think that higher education should be free while conservative-minded individuals in the USA might disagree.

Step Two then requires the two groups to find a specific example of someone (a politician perhaps) commenting one way or the other about the issue. The exact quote then becomes the answer to Step Two. Step Two should be done all together. This is critically important in order for the two sides to proceed. This is very different from real life in which opposing camps frequently begin their discussion about their very different perceptions rather than about a specific comment.

6

DIVING DEEPER INTO STEP TWO

Archer divides observations into two categories. She writes:

> Now that you know more about culture bumps and perceptions, the next step is to be able to tell the difference between a culture bump and the resulting perception. While it is somewhat artificial, it is useful to label these as descriptive observations and judgmental observations. A descriptive observation is one in which the event is described with no interpretation added (a report of exactly what happened), while a judgmental observation reflects the viewpoint of the observer. One way of testing whether or not an observation is judgmental is to ask the question, "Would I know that without being inside the head or heart of the other person?" If the answer is yes, the observation is descriptive; if the answer is no, then the observation is judgmental. This ability to separate is more easily said than done. A great deal of practice and self-motivation is required to become proficient.[23]

SECTION 3

STEP THREE: DESCRIBE WHAT YOU DID

The objective of Step Three is to become aware of your own action(s) and to describe these behavior(s) without judgment or interpretation.

7

STEP THREE: DESCRIBE WHAT YOU DID *(OR TELL IT LIKE IT WAS)*

While Step Three—like Step Two—is concerned with paying attention to how we describe behavior, it differs because the focus is on our own actions. If we think about describing our own actions at all—and we rarely do—such descriptions generally register as a combination of our feelings and our thoughts. Some examples are:

- "I didn't do anything"
- "What do you mean 'what did I do?' This isn't about me. It's about him/her/them/it!"
- "I was just minding my own business when s/he/it/they__________"
- "I was horrified at what I saw."

Unaware of Ourselves

In reality, we are amazingly unconscious about our own actions. We have only to apply Carspecken's objective, subjective or normative validity claims to the statements listed above to see that we are less conscious of our behavior than we are of other people's actions. In Step Three, we are asked to practice a truly counter-intuitive response to a culture bump; we are asked to look at ourselves objectively. And in Step Three, we realize that with ourselves, we frequently see nothing at all.

Separating Our Actions from Our Perceptions and Emotions

We realize that when we remember an incident, we generally recall how the other person(s) acted, looked or sounded. Any recollection of our participation in the incident usually revolves around how we felt at the time. While the culture bump approach includes understanding our own emotions about the incident in Step Four, in Step Three we deliberately and consciously focus on an objective description of our physical response in the incident. And as we recall from Step Two, an objective description is one that everyone, everywhere agrees about—a fact. As we untangle our own and the other person's actions from our perceptions, we take the first step in being able to understand ourselves. And understanding ourselves is essential if we want to increase our cross-cultural opportunities; knowing our basic reactions to situations allows us to choose new patterns, if we wish to do so.

We can only make an authentic and impartial analysis of the culture bump IF we approach it through an objective description. Therefore, in the language of reconstructive analysis, Steps Two and Three of the Culture Bump Protocol provide a structured way in which individuals experiencing a culture bump lay out their objective claims about the situation—in other words, tell exactly what happened.

If the first step, pinpoint the culture bump, is the driver of a micro-cultural approach, the second step and third step are the fulcrum of discovering our own truth.

The objective of Step Three is to become self-aware and describe our own actions without judgment or interpretation.

8

STEPPING INTO ACTION—DESCRIBE WHAT YOU DID

In Step Three, you describe exactly what you did—using only precise and literal descriptive language.

So now you might be asking yourself, exactly how do I "work" Step Three? How do I describe my own behavior? While it is somewhat artificial, you report exactly what happened with no interpretation. If we examine Step Three in our stories, we can see what this looks like.

In the first case study, Joy reports

> "I laughed and looked at Miguel and my friend."

In the second case study, Steven and his friends say,

> "Steve pointed to the box and said, 'What's that?' We all looked at the box."

In the third case study, Mike says,

> "I looked at him until he left the sanctuary then I looked back at the preacher."

In the fourth case study, Janice says,

> "I looked at him and said, 'No.'"

In the last case study, Carol says,
"I read the quote."

Notice that each of the sentences above use action words that describe a precise behavior. These words are *laughed, looked, pointed, said, left, read.*
Also notice that the action words are in the past tense since they describe what previously happened.

Now all you have to do is complete the following question, using precise, action words:

*What did I do or say?*____________________________________

More suggestions on HOW TO DO STEP THREE
What did I do

INSTRUCTIONS

1. Keep it simple.
2. One way of testing whether or not your observation is judgmental is to ask the question, "Would someone else see or know that without being inside my head or my heart?" If the answer is yes, the observation is descriptive; if the answer is no, then the observation is judgmental. You began developing this skill in Step Two and continue in this step. As you have probably noticed, this ability to separate is more easily said than done.
3. Another test is to ask whether your observation could have more than one interpretation. If the answer is yes, then it is probably objectively descriptive. For example, when Joy says, "I laughed and looked at Miguel and my friend" could be interpreted as being "cynical, fearful, or happy." In other words, the objective description could be verified by any other person.

CAUTIONS

- **Do** keep this very, very simple.
- **Don't** tell why you did anything in this step.
- **Don't** explain why you did anything in this step. You may recall some other small movements such as opening your eyes or taking a step forward or backward. Don't tell why you opened your eyes

("in surprise") or took a step backward ("in fear"). You will deal with your motivation and emotions in later steps.

- **Don't** add how you felt or your thoughts about the other person.

Special instructions for groups with opposing points of view.

Groups from different "camps"—whether they be political parties, religions or age groups—must first agree to use the culture bump steps about a specific incident that one side will experience as a "bump" while the incident is completely acceptable to the other side. *The primary difference between the way groups with disparate opinions actually apply the steps is whether they do the steps with one another or separately. Fundamentally, we need to be conscious of* ***what*** *we say,* ***when*** *we say it and* ***with whom*** *we say it.*

Group analysis of culture bumps

In this third step, each person in each group tells what he or she did when—as a group they listened to or read the specific issue. In this case, all will probably have the same answer—we listened to Senator________ speak or we read what Ms.________ said. This is quite simple.

Step Three should be done all together. This is critically important in order for the two sides to proceed. This is very different than in real life in which opposing camps frequently only discuss their very different perceptions rather than breaking the issue down together.

9

DIVING DEEPER INTO STEP THREE

All of the information about descriptive and judgmental observations that we practiced in Step Two is applicable in Step Three. However, there is an additional element that is more pertinent in Step Three than in Step Two that impacts people from different cultures. Archer explains:

> Some cultures allow for little reflection, while other cultures include as part of their shared interpretive frame, the notion of the usefulness of self-examination. In the latter type of cultures, e.g. Western cultures, this step may be more intuitive than in other types of cultures such as Asian. However, the separating of actual descriptive statements from those tinged with bias will be equally alien to all cultures.[24]

SECTION 4

STEP FOUR: LIST THE EMOTIONS YOU FELT WHEN THE BUMP HAPPENED

The objective of Step Four is to recall and re-experience our feelings so as to manage our emotions and "unhook" from the culture bump.

10

STEP FOUR: LIST THE EMOTIONS YOU FELT WHEN THE BUMP HAPPENED *(OR BRINGING IT ALL TOGETHER)*

With Step Four, we complete the first stage of the Culture Bump Protocol and unhook ourselves from our culture bump. While Steps Two and Three are concerned with paying attention to how we describe observable actions, Step Four moves into the realm of emotions. In Step Three, we focused on only our own actions, and likewise, in Step Four, we focus only on our own emotional response. In reality, if we think about our own emotions at all, they generally register as a combination of our feelings and our thoughts such as:

- "I felt like he was a bully"
- "I felt normal!"
- "I felt tired and hungry."
- "I felt really upset."
- "She made me crazy."

Step Four is an exercise in developing the ability to manage our emotional response or emotional intelligence and is the last step in achieving personal detachment from the culture bump itself. It may seem strange to think that we don't understand our own emotions but upon closer examination, we find that this is often the case. Archer writes about the difficulty in managing our emotions:

> The truth is that much of the time, we are unaware of our emotions, but we "react" to them anyhow. So, we begin by defining exactly what an emotion is. An emotion is a feeling that is accompanied by thoughts and physical reactions. These thoughts and physical reactions may be conscious or unconscious. While emotions are important in all areas of life, in cross-cultural communication, emotions play a very big role in how perceptions are formed. And perceptions influence how well we can form relationships with individuals who are different from ourselves. Therefore, in successful cross-cultural communication, we need to have knowledge about our own and other people's behaviors. But we also need to be "emotionally intelligent."[25]

True Emotions

And emotional intelligence is exactly what is needed in order to repair the primary break in our relationship with the other person(s). As Archer writes above, being able to identify a feeling is the first step. None of the examples at the beginning of this chapter are true emotions. "I felt like he was a bully" is a perception or opinion about someone else. However, the feeling I might have when I see a bully is probably fear or anger. In the same way, "normal" is an opinion (perhaps shared by some other people) but is not a feeling. Both "tired" and "hungry" are descriptions of a physical state. The precise meaning of "feeling upset" might be angry, fear or irritated or a combination of all of these feelings. In the Diving Deeper section of this chapter, there is a list of categories of emotions as compiled by Daniel Goleman in his book, Emotional Intelligence that can help identify many nuances of emotion.[26]

The Importance of Achieving Detachment

So, the combined intention of the first four steps is to achieve a sense of detachment. Once we are detached from the culture bump itself, we can analyze the experience in Steps Five through Seven. Therefore, in Steps One through Four, we are simultaneously detaching from our bump as well as consciously training our minds in a precise procedure for how to detach. Archer and Nickson explain this more fully below:

> Participants come to understand their own reaction to culture bumps by using the Eight Steps to analyze one of their own bumps. In learning the Eight Steps, the participants are actually acquiring three fundamental skills necessary for effective cross-cultural communication: (1) the skill of detaching, (2) the skill of identifying one's own cultural positioning as being relative, and (3) the skill of finding universal meaning in any situation. These skills are learned as follows:
> Steps One, Two, Three and Four teach participants how to detach by first identifying the culture bump, giving a precise description of the difference, and finally by expressing one's emotional response to the incident. The self-reflection required in these steps results in a sense of "detachment."[27]

Archer defines detachment as "describing the incident from at least two perspectives and separating the feelings from the behaviors and perceptions of the individual(s) impacted by the bump."[28]

Relationship Between the First Four Steps and Self-confidence

Archer and Nickson compared three case studies using the Culture Bump Approach and found that the first four steps are a guided pathway to self-reflection and self-confidence. An analysis of the data collected for this study suggested that self-confidence stems from separating the behavior from its emotional impact as practiced in Steps One through Four. The study further suggests that this detachment from the culture bump may result in an easier acceptance of different value systems. They state,

> Implicit in many of the participants' comments is a sense of empowerment that ranges from an awareness of having language to express the 'awkward feeling' accompanying a culture bump to having a step-by-step structure for processing the emotional, cognitive, and normative consequences of their own authentic experiences.[29]

Indeed, if the first step, pinpoint the culture bump, is the linchpin of a micro-cultural approach, the second step and third step are the pivot points to a new road of understanding ourselves and others, then the fourth step is the cornerstone of authentic self-awareness.

The objective of Step Four is to recall and re-experience our feelings in order to manage our emotions and "unhook" from the culture bump.

11

STEPPING INTO ACTION—LIST YOUR EMOTIONS

In Step Four, you recall, re-experience and list your emotions at the moment that you had the culture bump.

So now you might be asking yourself, exactly how do I "work" Step Four? How do I list my own feelings? There are four steps to listing your feelings.

1. Recall the incident that you identified in Step One. To the best of your ability, try to allow the emotions you experienced at that time, to re-surface.
2. Begin the list by deciding if your first emotion was surprise, shock or stunned. These are always the first feelings simply because the bump is not what you expected. If the bump was less impactful, you probably felt surprised, and felt shocked and stunned for more severe bumps.
3. Try to identify as many emotions as possible. NOTE: Some emotions may contradict one another. This is normal. Continue to list emotions until you find the most "tender" emotion.
4. Use emotion words rather than description words. In the examples at the beginning of this chapter, most of the words are description words—"normal," "tired," "upset." Do NOT write about the other person. Two examples of writing about the other person are:

    1) "I felt like he was really a bully"

2) "She made me crazy"

If we examine Step Four in our case studies, we can see what this step looks like.

In the first story, Joy recalls,
"I felt surprised, relieved, tickled and uncertain."

In the second story, Steven and friends say, (Each one might have a different set of emotions) but one said,
"We were surprised, curious and confused."

In the third story Mike says,
"I felt very surprised, curious, a little nervous and confused."

In the fourth story, Janice says,
"I felt surprised, angry, invisible and unsure."

In the case of Carol's culture bump with a politician, she says,
"I felt stunned, angry, fearful, sad, hopeless and despairing. I was shocked at my emotions."

Now all you have to do is complete the following question/sentence:

*At the time of the bump, the emotions I felt were:*________________________.

More suggestions on HOW TO DO STEP FOUR
List my emotions at the time of the bump

INSTRUCTIONS

1. Stay on this step long enough to re-experience as many emotions as possible.
2. There is always one "tender" emotion that allows you to "unhook" from the incident.
3. Try to use ordinary-life words such as "mad" rather than "angry"—or even "stupid" rather than "inadequate." The intention is to authentically re-experience the emotion for yourself.
4. Many times, anger is the feeling we are aware of, but if you "drill

down" below the anger, there will be another more "tender" emotion such as fear or sadness.

5. If you are bilingual, use your dominant language to begin the list. However, some words may be in your second language also.

CAUTIONS

- **Do** spend enough time on this step to really drill down to your deep emotions.
- **Don't** skim over it. You will actually feel a "release" from the bump when you identify all of your emotions.
- **Don't** use the terms "felt like," "felt that" or "felt about."
- **Don't** use terms like "She made me" or "They let me." In other words, don't begin with a focus on anyone other than yourself. These are descriptions about others rather than true feelings of your own.
- **Don't** use emotion words for physical states such as tired or hungry.

Special instructions for groups with opposing points of view.

Groups from different "camps"—whether they be political parties, religions or age groups—must first agree to use the culture bump steps about a specific incident that one side will experience as a "bump" while the incident is completely acceptable to the other side. *The primary difference between the way groups with disparate opinions actually apply the steps is whether they do the steps with one another or separately. Fundamentally, we need to be conscious of* ***what*** *we say,* ***when*** *we say it and* ***with whom*** *we say it.*

Group analysis of a culture bump

*Individual: I felt*____________

(NOTE: Each person lists his or her feelings separately and then shares those answers with others in the group)

*For example: I felt*__________________ *when I heard (or read) what So & So said.*

Group Analysis for groups with opposing viewpoints

In this fourth step, the two opposing sides MUST meet separately. This is critically important in order for the two sides to proceed. This is very different from real life in which both camps genuinely believe their own emotions are valid and noble while attributing objectionable emotions to the other side.

Therefore, this step has particular importance when working with two groups with opposing viewpoints. It is essentially an emotional mirroring process that is critical to the success of their eventually finding a common ground. Each of us has a set of emotions around controversial issues, and we intuitively share them with like-minded people. While this is necessary and normal, in real life, this is the only reaction most people have. We associate and talk with people who agree with us. If we talk to people who disagree, neither we nor they seem to be able to go beyond certain "sticking points"—mostly highly charged "sticking points."

In the Culture Bump Approach, these first four steps allow both sides to "vent" their emotions but provide a path out of the emotional morass with the fifth through eighth steps.

Essentially, each group is "mirroring" their emotional response to a "hot button" issue with their "own people." In this case, there will be a variety of emotions—even among folks with the same point of view.

Cautions for opposing groups

- **Do** manage your emotions
- **Don't** assume that you are right simply because like-minded people share your emotional response.
- **Don't** expect the "opposing team" to share your feelings. Share your feelings with like-feeling folks.
- **Don't** talk—at this point—about any issues. Just limit your discussion to your emotions.

12

DIVING DEEPER INTO STEP FOUR

In the previous three steps, we have been scrupulous about not allowing our emotions to color the descriptions of our own or of others' behavior. However, in step four, we focus exclusively on the emotional aspect of our bump.

The first step in emotional intelligence is to be able to know what you are feeling when you are feeling it. Sometimes in the middle of a culture bump, you may not be aware of your feelings. But, afterwards, you can recall the many emotions you felt and name them. This will help you to see things from other people's emotional point of view.

This is very important in cross-cultural communication since many times our response to people who are different is to "feel" that they are inferior or that they are "superior." Another typical feeling is fear or sadness, which is "covered" with anger or indifference. Below are clusters of emotions with their nuances. These are only a few of the hundreds and hundreds of emotions.

ANGER

Fury, resentment, exasperation, indignation, irritability, annoyance, hatred

SADNESS

Grief, sorrow, melancholy, self-pity, dejection, despair

FEAR
Anxiety, nervous, concern, wariness, panic, terror

ENJOYMENT
Happy, joy, relief, contentment, delight, satisfied, euphoria

LOVE
Acceptance, trust, kindness, connectedness, adoration, infatuation

SURPRISE
Shock, astonishment, amazement, wonder

DISGUST
Contempt, disdain, scorn, aversion distaste

SHAME
Guilt, embarrassment, chagrin remorse, humiliation, regret, mortification[30]

5

STEP FIVE: FIND THE UNIVERSAL SITUATION IN THE CULTURE BUMP

The objective of Step Five is to identify at least one universal situation embodied in the culture bump.

13

STEP FIVE: FIND THE UNIVERSAL SITUATION IN THE INCIDENT WHEN IT HAPPENED *(OR STEPPING OUTSIDE)*

In the first four steps, we have been remembering and re-constructing what happened in order to "unhook" ourselves from the bump. If we do not detach from our experience of the bump in this way, it is very difficult for us to see anything more than the "odd" behavior of the other person(s). However, by disentangling ourselves in the first four steps, in Steps Five through Eight, we move progressively farther and farther from the culture bump itself and deeper into our own expectations. In other words, we self-reflected about what "they" did, what we did and how we felt about it. Now we *global-reflect* about the incident. We begin this *global-reflection* by thinking about the universal aspect of our culture bump. Specifically, in steps five and six we examine our own cultural actions in a universal situation—in other words, we examine our own cultural relativism.

Same Situations Exist for All Human Beings

We begin by thinking about the universality of our culture bump. We first consider the fact that, rarely, if ever, do we humans do anything that other human beings around the globe do not also do. We eat, greet, lie to, make deals with, give advice to, and become angry with one another all around the world. However, what we eat, how we eat, when we eat or with whom we eat varies from group to group and even individual to individual. But, fundamentally, we are all just eating. In the same way, we all greet one another by:

- shaking hands,
- high fiving,
- nodding,
- bowing,
- smiling,
- fist-bumping (with swish and without swish),
- hugging,
- not hugging,
- looking one another in the eyes
- looking at the floor

...depending on who we are, where we are, whom we are greeting, where we come from, our age, our status, how we feel etc. We all lie (or fib) to others but how we lie, to whom we lie, how we think about our lie, what we lie about, why we lie—all depend on an endless number of motivations. And business people around the globe know that deal-making depends on and reflects cultural values. What is common to all of these human interactions is that they share basic situations such as acknowledging one another's presence, making a deal, protecting ourselves or others, feeding our bodies, etc. The billions of situations in which we humans find ourselves daily can be expanded indefinitely.

Archer gives a few examples of common situations worldwide.

- Female saying "No" to a male's invitation
- Letting a member of the opposite sex know you are interested in him/her; flirting behavior
- Asking for a favor from a (1) superior or an (equal)
- Being part of a community of people; feeling connected to a group
- Wanting to help another person or people
- Being inspired; having goals and hopes
- Showing respect to a person who is (1) older (2) younger (3) same age
- Being in a situation where you are bored/uncomfortable/scared but cannot extricate yourself.[31]

Relationship Between Universals and Function in Language

Language is another way to try to understand universal situations. Our words always express a fundamental idea. For example, the basic idea of *a friend giving advice* can be expressed with different words such as,

"You should_____,"

"It would be a good idea to______"

"Do _____," or

"You might want to think about_____."

In this case, a friend giving advice is the universal situation and the exact words are different ways of expressing that particular universal circumstance. The exact words chosen depend on the situation, the culture, the individual and the group, etc. In everyday life, we only pay attention to the different ways of speaking without ever consciously thinking about the universal situation.

Relationship Between Universals and Connection

In fact, Archer states that "while we rarely reflect on the universal notions or situations implicit in our daily interactions, they are the foundation for a thorough analysis of those interactions. And while theorizing about the motivation for a particular 'odd' behavior seems to be innate, framing the answer as a universal situation is not."[32] Although reflection about commonalities is rare, Abdallah-Pretceille insists it is critical in order to bring differences toward a subjacent universality where reconnection occurs. She acknowledges that looking at differences is easier than reflecting on commonalities, but asserts that without this reflection, our focus on "differences" or bumps simply leads "to cultural dead-ends, by overemphasizing cultural differences and by enhancing, consciously or otherwise, stereotypes or even prejudices."[33] Abdallah-Pretceille does not tell us exactly how she believes we must reflect in order to arrive at a "subjacent universality," but Gadamer suggests that reflection is circular in nature—meaning that we need to understand the detail in terms of the whole and the whole in terms of the detail. And Archer points out that Gadamer's circle:

> ...is inherent in the culture bump process. The culture bump begins with a specific incident (detail) and proceeds to extrapolate a universal situation out of it (whole) It then moves on to examine one individual's expectations of a specific cultural behavior (detail) and relates that to a world

> view norm (whole). The whole process is repeated by questioning an individual from the other culture as to how he or she perceives the universal quality (whole). It can thus be seen that this secondary process then again begins with a whole and moves to a detail or the second individual's expectations of a specific cultural behavior.[34]

Therefore, however, counter-intuitive it is to think of our daily activities as being universal, Step Five always opens a door to our glimpsing our fundamental connection to everyone everywhere—without exception. And this glimpse is essential to continuing with Steps Six and Seven and ultimately to a conversation for common ground.

The objective of Step Five is to extricate at least one universal situation out of the culture bump and in so doing, become emotionally aware that people around the world face the same situations.

14

STEPPING INTO ACTION—IDENTIFY AT LEAST ONE UNIVERSAL SITUATION

In Step Five, you drill down to the universal situation in the culture bump.

So now you might be asking yourself, exactly how do I "work" Step Five? How do I find a universal situation in my culture bump? There are two parts to finding at least one universal situation.

1. We recall the definition of our culture bump in Step 2. It will always be one of four things: (1) the exact words that someone said or wrote, (2) an observable action, (3) the way someone said something or (4) an object. These four types of bumps are invariably a response to a particular situation or circumstance. The situation itself can exist anywhere in the world while the responses (or bumps) are specific to a culture, a group or an individual. For example, eating food is a universal situation but using fingers, chopsticks or spoons are some of the many responses to the universal situation of *eating food.*
2. Ask yourself (or someone who might have more information than you) why the other person acted as they did. The objective with this question is not to "understand" the other person(s)' motive but to identify the situation to which they were responding. This will lead you to a type of universal. Interestingly, there may be more than one answer—depending on the source of your information. You can refine the answer by adding details. For

example, what were the roles of the individuals involved, the ages, pertinent relationships, gender, or did the situation occur in public or in private.

We can understand these three steps better by looking at how Joy, Mike and Steven arrived at the universal situations in their culture bumps.

In Joy's case,

1. She recalls that Miguel tells Karen, "So you are an international girlfriend."
2. When Joy asked other Venezuelans about Miguel's response, they confirmed that his comment about being an international girlfriend was indeed typical and showed that he was being empathetic.

She then asks herself "why" he had made the comment. Rather than accepting her intuitive answer—"He was being critical or being nice"—she focuses on what had elicited his comment. In other words, what did Karen do or say that prompted his response. Joy recalls that Karen said that she had dated more than one man at the same time—and considers the fact that Karen is older than Miguel and doesn't know him well. Therefore, she is revealing information about herself that is sensitive. As Joy thinks about this, she realizes that revealing sensitive information about oneself is something that could happen anywhere in the world to anyone. However, the precise way that people respond to self-revelations may vary by culture, age, gender, and many other factors.

So, she identifies one universal situation as:

Responding to someone who has revealed sensitive information about themselves.

In Mike's case,

1. He recalls that Lawrence stood up and walked out of the church sanctuary while raising his right arm up in the air, with his index finger pointing straight up.
2. When Mike asked Lawrence about his behavior, Lawrence explained that he was excusing himself for a brief absence from the service. He further explained that holding the arm and index finger up was the custom in many African-American congregations when leaving a church service.

So, when Mike thinks about why Lawrence acted the way he did, he moves past his thoughts about Lawrence being mad to focus on what had elicited Lawrence's behavior. In other words, he focuses on what happened that prompted Lawrence's action.

He realizes that excusing oneself from a church service is not quite universal but that needing to briefly leave a gathering of people listening to a speaker is something that can happen anywhere in the world to anyone. However, the precise way that people respond to the need to briefly leave out from a gathering may vary by culture, age, gender and many other factors.

So, he identifies one universal situation in his culture bump as:

Needing to unexpectedly leave a gathering of people listening to a speaker.

In some ways, it is easier to find the universal situation in culture bumps that are objects, such as a donation box.

So in Steven's case,

1. He recalls that they saw a wooden box (5'x5'x5') with a tin roof and an opening in the front, situated on the street. On one side, it had writing that said, "Donations of clothing, shoes and toys."
2. When Steven checked the definition of the word "donations" in his Chinese/English dictionary, he knew the basic purpose for the box.

But since he still needed to know more about why Americans have boxes on the street for donations, he moves past his thoughts about Americans being kind or (foolish) and focuses on what had elicited the creation of such boxes. Like Joy, he double-checked his answer with several Americans who confirmed that the boxes were a typical way of helping people who needed clothes, shoes and other items. Even without the word donations, his asking Americans about the box would have given him the same information. As he talks with Americans, he realizes that people are putting things in the boxes to (1) eliminate surplus clothing and (2) to help people who need clothes or toys or shoes. So, he has two possible universal situations: eliminating surplus objects and helping people who are in need. Both of these situations can happen anywhere in the world to anyone. However, the precise way that people respond to the need to eliminate surplus objects or to helping people who are in need may vary by culture, age, gender and many other factors.

So he identifies one universal situation in his culture bump as:

Helping people who are in need

In summary, the culture bump (action, words or objects) is one of many possible responses to a situation that is universal.

Therefore, in the first story, Joy defines the universal situation as:

Responding to someone who has revealed sensitive information about themselves

In the second story, Steven and his friends say the universal situation is

Helping other people who are in need

In the third story, Mike says that the universal situation is

Needing to unexpectedly leave a gathering of people listening to a speaker

In the fourth story, Janice says that the universal situation is

Being excited and distracted by something when someone else is speaking."

In the case of Carol's culture bump with a politician, she says the basic situation is,

Ensuring a safe environment in a public place (such as a university.

Now all you have to do is complete the following instruction:

Find the universal situation in the incident.

*Why did the person(s) do what they did:*______________________________.

Remember that in asking why the person(s) did or said the "bump," you are not looking for their personal motivation; you are looking for the situation that prompted their words or actions.

More suggestions on HOW TO DO STEP FIVE
Find the universal situation in the incident

INSTRUCTIONS

1. Stay on this step long enough to find a fairly specific situation.
2. Remember this is a situation—not a quality. You will look for

qualities in Step Seven.

3. Focus on the fact that every cultural/personal difference has something that is universal.
4. Become conscious that everybody around the world shares the same situations.

CAUTIONS

- The situation is never "normal."
- Don't worry too much about the "perfect" situation. There are always more than one situation in any culture bump. Anyone will work. You cannot find a wrong situation.

Special instructions for groups with opposing points of view.

The primary difference between the way groups with disparate opinions actually apply the steps is whether they do the steps with one another or separately. Fundamentally, we need to be conscious of ***what*** *we say,* ***when*** *we say it and* ***with whom*** *we say it.*

Step Five is always done together. The two groups will have managed their emotions separately before coming back together to find a universal or common situation. This is the first opportunity for the opposing sides to come to an agreement together. Needless to say, the universal must truly be universal for both sides to agree.

Group analysis of culture bumps

We agree that the universal situation underlying (blank) saying (blank) is_______.

Group Analysis for groups with opposing viewpoints

In this fifth step, the two opposing sides MUST meet together. This is critically important in order for the two sides to proceed.

Cautions for opposing groups

- **Do** continue to manage your emotions.
- **Don't** try to make points in this step.
- **Don't** talk, at this point, about any specific issues. Just limit your discussion to finding a universal situation or situations. If there are more than one situation, simply choose one with which to continue your analysis.

15

DIVING DEEPER INTO STEP FIVE

As Archer points out:

> Commonalities exist in two ways- they can be (1) common situations such as "finishing an exam before the time is finished" or they can be (2) common qualities such as "being a good student", "cheating", "showing off", "modesty" and "risk taking." In step five, we are concerned only with identifying the common situation.

Every culture bump - every different action that we encounter - has both of these aspects. Embedded in every behavior is both a condition that is common to all humanity and an assumption of a shared meaning attached to that action. Understanding this provides a foundation for our intuitive belief that "we are all just human". It also provides a specific strategy for finding common ground with all of our relationships—with people from different religions, different professions, different families - even with our spouses and siblings!

While we face thousands of situations on a daily basis and choose from multiple possible responses to those situations, we are usually unconscious of any of them. It is only when our culture bumps provide an opportunity to stop and pay attention that we can self-reflect about our own behaviors and intentions. And in that self-reflection, we come to understand ourselves at a more profound level and use what we find out about ourselves to connect to one another beyond cultural and personal divisions.[35]

SECTION 6

STEP SIX: DESCRIBE WHAT YOU WOULD DO OR WOULD EXPECT OTHERS TO DO IN THAT UNIVERSAL

The objective of Step Six is to recall and describe precisely your expected behavior in the universal situation identified in Step Five.

16

STEP SIX: DESCRIBE WHAT YOU WOULD DO OR WOULD EXPECT OTHERS TO DO IN THAT UNIVERSAL SITUATION *(OR NORMAL IS JUST A SETTING ON A WASHING MACHINE)*

With Step Six, we complete the second stage of the Culture Bump Protocol and discover that our own actions are culturally relative. In other words, we discover that our behavior, while normal for us, is only one pattern among many other patterns. Just as we did in Step Two, in this sixth step, we are describing behavior in a specific situation. However, in Step Two, we only had to recall our action in our personal culture bump, while in Step Six we need to recall one or more patterns of behavior of how we habitually respond in the particular circumstance identified in Step Five.[36]

Unfortunately, this is not intuitive. In fact, our usual response to Step Six generally registers as either a judgment or as opposition thoughts. When asked what we would do in a particular situation, we tend to say things like:

"Well, in that situation,

- I just act normal (or)
- I use common sense (or)
- I am respectful (or)
- I certainly don't do what s/he/they do! (or)
- Well it depends (or)

- What do you mean? Everybody knows what to do in that situation!"

Cultural Blind Spots

It seems that we human beings are amazingly unconscious about the specific behaviors that we habitually do and that we expect others to do. Hall's early insight that our primary task is to come to understand ourselves rather than understanding others is amplified by Bernstein who asserts that "individuals may have not only occasional false beliefs about what they are doing, but systematically distorted misconceptions of themselves, the meaning of their actions and their historical situations."[37,38]

Other scholars have written extensively about the need to overcome our cultural blind-spots. For example, Jurgen Habermas tells us that one way to overcome our blind-spots is by understanding the yardstick we use for our normal behavior—in other words to understand our expectations.[39] Archer defines the word expectation as used in Step Six as a range of behaviors that exists between two culturally defined parameters. More specifically, it includes all those behaviors—both appropriate and inappropriate—that we unconsciously assume that we or others like us will do in a specific situation.[40]

So, in Step Six, we examine the pattern of our behaviors for members of our identity group in the generalized universal situation identified in Step Five. For example, the words at the beginning of this chapter, *normal, common sense and respectful*, are indicative of what the speakers assume about the typical behavior for a group of people. The words reflect what that group of people assume to be a "fact." So, Step Six, like Steps Two and Three, calls for separating our subjective thoughts (meaning they are based on my interpretation rather than a fact) or normative thoughts (meaning they are based on my community's idea of what is a fact) from that group's typical objective, observable behaviors. So, in Step Six we tell exactly what we expect of ourselves and others.

The Importance of Mirroring

Because we are examining a broader pattern of behavior than our original culture bump, an integral part of Step Six is our intuitive need to "mirror." Archer defined mirroring as "checking out one's intercultural experience with members of one's own culture." In other words, we intuitively talk about our experiences with folks that think like we do. She noted that mirroring can be the breeding ground for stereotype formation when individuals from the same culture reinforce one another's interpretation of a cultural difference.[41] This is precisely what occurs on social media when like-minded people share and post their own points of view to others who share the same view. Any alternative views are deleted or dismissed. Therefore, divisiveness is encouraged, enhanced and reinforced. But even without social media, we are not wired to self-reflect about ourselves. As Archer wrote about encountering difference:

> it is examined from the point of view that "they/he/she" are different rather than "I/we" are different. If we discuss the incident, we almost always do so with individuals from our own culture.... And as a result, are confirmed in our impressions of the other. Thus, are the seeds of a stereotype sown.[42]

Prejudice and Behavioral Bias

As opposed to everyday life, in Step Six, "mirroring becomes a structured group self-reflection process about the nuances of one's own cultural expectations and evaluations. This group self-reflection allows shared cultural bias to become explicit."[43] Whether we "mirror" with others of our community about our various responses to Step Five's universal situation or simply replay our own past responses, we discover our cultural *Behavioral Bias* rather than regarding bias as a personal identity. It is what I do rather than who I am: its value is not in shaming or blaming us for being biased, but is rather an amazing self-awareness that borders on self-aweness. We regard our bias—not as right or wrong, justified or unjustified, better or worse—but as a unique expression of ourselves. Step Six becomes the fulfillment of Gadamer's assertion that our prejudice is precisely the way that we can understand other human beings.[44] We can understand why Archer states that:

> Culture bump theory builds on this (Gadamer's) perspective on prejudice by insisting, not on the elimination of but rather on the identification and acknowledgement of prejudices by removing them from the intersubjective, unconscious status in which they normally exist. This insight thereby provides the subtle shift that allows bias and ethnocentrism to become the key rather than a barrier to cross-cultural understanding.[45]

Step Six, by depending on our intuitive response of mirroring, actually brings our shared patterns of behavior out of the subjective realm of our minds into our consciousness. As we self-reflect and/or talk with other people from our community, we become aware of a multitude of our own cultural nuances and our sometimes-surprising reasons for different behaviors. Thus, we begin to see ourselves as being cultural—as opposed to being "normal." In other words, we experience being culturally relative and, in Hall's words, "Come to know our own culture."

From Behavioral Bias to Connection

Arriving at an understanding of our bias after managing our emotions in Step Four and acknowledging a subjacent universality in Step Five allows us to move beyond the defense and denial or self-flagellation that are our intuitive responses to seeing ourselves at this level. Archer and Nickson alluded to this new understanding of bias when they gave an explanation for why the experience of discovering our own bias through the Culture Bump Approach leads to healthy self-confidence and openness to other world views in their comparative studies of Culture Bump trainees:

> The Culture Bump Approach not only overtly reassures participants that the focus of the training is on forming human connections, but it also teaches them the skills necessary to find the commonalities with individuals from different cultures. It is possibly this conscientious focus on commonalities within differing cultural perceptions at the onset of the training that sets a tone of inclusiveness and security that ameliorates the defensiveness and minimization.... It may be that an individual's conscious awareness of common humanity while learning about cultural differences facilitates his or her passage through Bennett's (1986) developmental stages of intercultural sensitivity.[46]

In short, in Step Six, it is as though we look through a microscope into our blind spot at our biased behavior and discover that being our authentic selves is better than being right. Indeed, there is a comfort in standing with our feet firmly planted in Step Five's universality while moving the spotlight over our inner selves. We then look up and out with interest and curiosity about others' "cultural bias." Archer and Nickson point out the significance of this dispassionate view:

> This micro view shifts the focus from attempting to eliminate prejudice and ethnocentrism to acknowledging them as the source of personal, existential meaning. This acknowledgment is embodied in the sixth step, which then becomes the key for diverse individuals to truly connect with one another in a process that is both synergistic and transformational. This process of uncovering and sharing one's own cultural criteria for common human themes is the core of the Culture Bump Approach.[47]

The objective of Step Six is to recall and describe precisely our expected behavior in the universal situation in Step Five.

17

STEPPING INTO ACTION—DESCRIBE WHAT YOU WOULD DO OR WOULD EXPECT OTHERS TO DO IN THAT UNIVERSAL SITUATION.

In Step Six, you recall and objectively describe either your own or someone from your group's behavior in the situation identified in Step Five.

So now you might be asking yourself, exactly how do I "work" Step Six? How do I identify and describe one of my expected behaviors in the universal situation in Step Five? There are two parts to Step Six.

1. Begin with the situation that you identified in Step Five and then recall either your own behavior or that of someone from your own culture in that specific circumstance. It may help to think of a specific example of another person in that situation who acted in a way in which you approve.
2. Describe that action (or object) without adding any of your perceptions. In other words, use only descriptive language that would carry the same meaning to anyone outside of yourself. Describe exactly what happens (or would happen) without any of your or anyone else's viewpoint.

In summary, Step Six of the Culture Bump Protocol asks us to create a description of one or more patterns of behavior of how people in our own culture are expected to respond in the previously identified universal situation. This description could be verified by other members of our culture. If we examine Step Six in our stories, we see examples of these descriptions

In the first case, Joy reports

"When someone has revealed sensitive information about themselves, *I would either joke about it or self-reveal in turn.*"

In the second case study, Steven and his friends say,

"When Chinese people are in need, *we depend on Chinese companies and corporations to provide the bulk of charitable donations for building schools or for disasters.*"

In the third case study, Mike says,

"When I need to unexpectedly leave a gathering of people who are listening to a speaker, *I leave out as quietly as possible, making as little eye contact as possible. If I am with someone, I might whisper, 'I'll be back shortly.'*"

In the fourth case study, Janice says,

"What I do when I am excited and distracted by something when someone else is speaking? I may say, '*Wow look at that.....then say 'Sorry what were you saying?*'"

In the last case study, Carol says,

"How a society ensures a safe environment in a public place such as a university campus. I recalled instances at my university when there was concern about possible dangers. Administrators responded by *(1) having individuals sitting in classrooms or undercover campus police present at particular events and (2) Having alarm buttons on podiums as well as certain desks.*

Now complete the sentence below.

Identify and describe at least one of your expected behaviors in the situation identified in Step Five. ________________________________.

More suggestions on HOW TO DO STEP SIX
List my expectations for that universal situation

INSTRUCTIONS

1. If you cannot remember being in the exact situation, imagine what you would do if you ever found yourself in that or a similar position.
2. If possible, discuss the behaviors with someone from your own background or community.
3. Try to make the behavior as precise and vivid as possible—Add as many details as you can recall.
4. One way of testing whether or not your observation is judgmental is to ask the question, "Would someone else know that without being inside my head or my heart?" If the answer is yes, the observation is descriptive; if the answer is no, then the observation is judgmental. This ability to separate is more easily said than done.

   Another test is to ask whether your observation could have more than one interpretation. If the answer is yes, then it is probably objectively descriptive. For example, "I laughed and looked at Miguel and my friend" could be interpreted as being "cynical, fearful, or happy."

   In other words, the objective description could be verified by any other person.
5. The more you can define the nuances of the behavior, the more helpful this step will be.

CAUTIONS

- **Don't** skip over this step. Take time to think and discuss with other people as much as possible. Pay attention to any and all patterns of behavior that you see emerging.
- **Don't** focus on why you did anything in this step. You may recall some other small movements such as opening your eyes or taking a step forward or backward. Don't tell why you opened your eyes ("in surprise") or took a step backward ("in fear."). You will deal with your motivation and emotions in Step Seven.
- **Don't** compare your behavior to the other person's behavior in the culture bump! You are beyond the culture bump at this point!

Special instructions for groups with opposing points of view.

The primary difference between the way groups with disparate opinions actually apply the steps is whether they do the steps with one another or separately. Fundamentally, we need to be conscious of ***what*** *we say,* ***when*** *we say it and* ***with whom*** *we say it.*

Step Six is always done separately. After having agreed on the universal situation in the previous step, the groups separate and begin to define exactly what action they would like to see occur. There may be some disagreement—even within the group. This step is particularly important for working with two groups with opposing points of view. In this step, most people become conscious of their own ideas—perhaps for the first time. For example, Carol talks about becoming conscious about both her emotions and ideas when working on Step Six of her culture bump about guns on campus.

Once again, I was stumped. I realized that I really had no other response other than anger and frustration. But by acknowledging the depth of my emotions in Step Four, I found that I was able to begin to develop another response to the real situation and not just my response to guns. I realized that people carrying guns was actually one way to respond! But I also recalled incidents at the University of Houston when there was possible danger and the administration responded by having individuals sitting in classrooms or undercover campus police present at particular events. This triggered the insight that university could develop programs modeled on RA Programs (dormitory leaders). University police departments could assume responsibility for vetting and training student leaders in each department (perhaps utilizing ROTC units). In addition, university undercover officers could assume responsibility for specific buildings on campus. Alarm buttons on podiums as well as certain desks in classrooms could alert the entire system—all under the auspices of campus police.

When like-minded folks are obliged to discuss—in behavioral terms—their expectations, the result are specific solutions (including those with which we disagree) to the original bump. This provides a foundation for beginning a conversation in Step Eight with the group with opposing viewpoints and allows the two sides in Step Eight to keep their focus on solutions rather than proving themselves right (or the others wrong)

Group analysis of culture bumps

We would like to have the following action to help resolve the situation in step five.

________________________________.

Group Analysis for groups with opposing viewpoints

In this sixth step, the two opposing sides MUST meet separately. This is critically important.

Cautions for opposing groups

- Do continue to manage your emotions
- Do try to come up with specific actions that you think would be the correct solution(s) to the situation
- Don't talk about "Them"

18

DIVING DEEPER INTO STEP SIX

Diving deeper into Step Six, it is helpful to look at macro-cultural approaches to understanding differences but with micro-cultural eyes. Our culture bumps are the physical manifestation of something much deeper—our cultural values. In other words, our "bumps" or our differing behaviors come from the values that we hold dear in our culture. And, our values come from our national cultures, our regional cultures, our family culture and from our unique, personal culture. There are numerous macro-cultural models and theories that have been developed to explain these cultural differences. They generally divide cultures into individual-oriented and group-oriented cultures. One such model was developed by Pierre Cass. The difference can be visualized as a Staircase Model of Culture and a Rollercoaster Model of Culture.

In the Staircase model (which typifies many American values), the individual begins at the bottom and by hard work, moves up. The beliefs associated with this model are that individuals have control of their lives, individuals are responsible for their lives and that upward striving is desirable. The individual in this model would be competitive and ambitious. In contrast, in the Rollercoaster model, outside forces control the individual, and the individual has minimal control over his or her life. There is an emphasis on enjoyment of the present moment, and it doesn't matter how hard the individual works—there is only certainty of peaks and valleys in succession in the future.[48]

SECTION 7

STEP SEVEN: LIST THE QUALITIES YOU FEEL THAT ACTION DEMONSTRATES

The objective of Step Seven is to discern and name the precise meaning of the behavior described in Step Six.

19

STEP SEVEN: LIST THE QUALITIES THAT YOU FEEL THAT ACTION DEMONSTRATES *(OR WHY, OH WHY, DO I DO WHAT I DO?)*

Step Seven brings us to the third and final stage of the Culture Bump Protocol. We completed the first stage in Steps One through Four when we "unhooked" from our original culture bump. That detachment allowed us to uncover universal situations in Step Five and our expected conduct in Step Six. This awareness of our own cultural relativism moved us past thinking that "they are just like us" to begin to wonder if "I am like you." Throughout the steps, we have separated actions and perceptions and fully understand that there are meanings attached to actions. We have seen that when our own expectations are not met, we usually think the other person(s) is "wrong or possibly better" but always DIFFERENT. While these cultural insights are exciting, in Step Seven we shift from examining specific aspects of our own group identity into exploring our common humanity. If we think about being human or having common humanity, *and we rarely do,* such thoughts generally revolve around superficial comparisons with other groups of people or animals. We say things such as:

- "Well, everybody loves their families."
- "Everybody makes mistakes."
- "There is good and bad in all of us." OR
- "We humans are different from all other animals because we can

think and create. Look at how WE have changed through the centuries."

Multiple Layers of Knowledge

In reality, what we subconsciously think is that everybody loves their families the way I love my family. And my mistakes are truly mistakes; your mistakes, however, are just wrong. But in Step Six, we became conscious that love for family can have many forms. In other words, knowledge of the various ways that other people act in the same situation gave us one level of information that is needed to re-connect. But Archer explains that knowing about another culture requires different levels of knowledge. She says:

> The essence of the dilemma *(of re-connecting)* is that its solution is imperfectly identified as merely acquiring knowledge about the "culture bump" rather than acquiring the various levels of knowledge that must be grasped in order for re-connection to occur....There is a need for objective knowledge *(meaning everyone everywhere agrees about it—a fact)*....But in order for connection to re-occur or to be maintained, an individual needs to acquire, not only objective knowledge about a culture but evaluative*(meaning if people think it is good or bad)* and normative *(meaning the specific action people expect others to do).* Indeed, if he or she acquires only objective knowledge without concurrently acquiring the other culture's criteria with which to evaluate the behavior, and if that knowledge confirms very different patterns of behavior, the acquisition of such objective knowledge could even intensify or justify the feeling of disconnectedness.[49]

In other words, our purpose is to connect or re-connect with one another. And I need to know ***what*** you are doing, ***why*** you are doing it and ***how*** I would do it in order to truly connect to you.

We move through these various levels of understanding of ourselves and others in the 8 Step Protocol. The first level of universal meaning occurs in Step Five when we make universal situations explicit; Step Seven requires identifying the universal meaning associated with our own daily behavior. In other words, we take a deeper look at our own actions to identify the specific qualities or meanings that we assume they stand for. One way to tackle "meaning" is by grappling with our personal interpretation when life unfolds as we expect. Again, when we are asked what it means to us when our expectations are met, we generally respond:

- Well, it just feels right
- You know, normal.

Looking Beyond Normal

But Step Seven requires drilling beyond the rightness of our "feeling" to what those specific qualities are that makes it feel normal. As Archer succinctly put it, "When people in my culture (do the behavior in Step Six), I say they are__________." And normal is never the right answer! Because we are being asked to uncover the implicit or implied value which that behavior in that situation carries in our own culture, "mirroring" with members of our own group allows everyone to gradually bring into focus exactly what it means to us when we do what we do. In fact, we begin to uncover the layers and layers through which we see the world. We begin to "escape the hidden restraints of our culture" by making explicit the nuances of our culturally shared knowledge.[50]

Finding Deep Human Culture

We examine and pick out the threads of meaning that run through these minute—even trivial—behaviors that we typically never question. And as we grapple with finding our own unspoken meaning embedded in what we do, we move into the deep structure of human culture—the culture of being human rather than the culture of being American, French or Japanese, old, young, or middle-aged, liberal or conservative or even male and female. And we discover that an unknown and astonishing human connection always exists at the level of meaning.

With Step Seven, we understand all culture—including our own to be foreign—and our subjacent human culture to be our own true culture.

The objective of Step Seven is to discern and name the meaning or precise qualities of the behavior described in Step Six.

20

STEPPING INTO ACTION—FIND THE MEANING OR PRECISE QUALITIES IN THE ACTION DESCRIBED IN STEP SIX

So now you might be asking yourself, exactly how do I "work" Step Seven? How do I find *meaning* in actions? Remember you are looking for a quality that all human beings possess. Many of these are subtle, everyday qualities that we take for granted. Some examples of qualities could be things like *sincere* or *cynical, spunky* and *fearful, cool* or *tacky*—the more precise, the better. Note that in this step "quality" does not mean good or bad; it means an attribute that is ascribed to a specific behavior. We assume it is a characteristic of people who behave in this particular way. There are several layers to working this step. The first layer is to use your imagination

1. Begin to identify this human quality by imagining yourself (or other people from your cultural group) doing the behavior described in Step Six.
2. The second layer is to ask yourself how you felt in that situation. Another question would be to ask yourself what kind of person do you believe would do that behavior?
3. Another way to find the quality is to identify the opposite quality if your expectations are not met. Again, ask yourself, what kind of person does that behavior? A third question is to ask yourself, when have I demonstrated ________ (that quality I accuse them of

being).

For example, in our first story, Joy says,

> "When I asked other Venezuelans if they thought his comment about international girlfriend was typical, they said that not only was it typical, but it meant that he was trying to be empathetic with her. So, then she imagined herself or other Americans' behavior in response to someone revealing sensitive information about themselves" (The universal situation identified in Step Five).

She first imagines Americans doing what Miguel did—joking. He said, "So you are an international girlfriend and I thought it was funny" (Step One—what I thought about the culture bump). And she identifies the meaning for her when Americans do what (Miguel) as alluding to the darker side of the action while not exactly criticizing it.

So, she has now identified "being critical" as the universal quality she had unconsciously ascribed to Miguel's behavior.

Critical.

She continues with imagining what she (or other) Americans do. However, when I or many other Americans self-reveal as a response, I think I am being empathetic (Step Seven—meaning of behavior). She has now identified 'being empathetic" as the universal quality she unconsciously ascribes for herself (or people like her.) She also realizes that she is unclear about the full meaning of "empathy" from the Venezuelan perspective.

Empathetic

Critical and empathetic are qualities that exist for all human beings.

We can understand Step Seven better by looking at all of our stories.

As noted above, Joy says,

> "When I or someone in my culture, self-reveals as a response to someone revealing sensitive information about themselves, I say **we are empathetic."**

In the second story, Steven and his friends said,

> "When we depend on Chinese companies to provide the bulk of charitable donations for building schools or for disasters, we say that

we are being compassionate."

In the third story, Mike says,

"When I unexpectedly leave a gathering of people who are listening to a speaker as quietly as possible, making as little eye contact as possible and whispering to anyone I am with, 'I'll be back shortly,' **I think I am being considerate to the other people there at the event and to the speaker."**

In the fourth story, Janice says,

"When I am excited and distracted by something when someone else is speaking and may say, 'Wow look at that.....then say 'Sorry what were you saying?,' **I think I am showing the other person I care about them."**

And Carol says,

"When I imagine ensuring a safe environment by specific actions such as the administrators having individuals sitting in classrooms or undercover campus police present at particular events, **I say we are being hopeful and creative in problem solving."**

Now complete the following sentence. Reflect on and articulate your meaning you would feel or think about the action you identified in Step Six.

*When people in my culture (group) do (fill in the behavior listed in Step Six), I say they are*____.

More suggestions on HOW TO DO STEP SEVEN
Find the meaning for me when my expectations are met

INSTRUCTIONS

1. If you cannot remember being in the exact situation, imagine how you would feel or think if you ever found yourself in that or a similar circumstance.
2. If possible, discuss the action with someone from your own background or community.
3. Sometimes this conversation will trigger other insights about yourself or your community.
4. The more you can define the various nuances of the behavior, the more helpful this step will be.

5. Steps Six and Seven shift our focus from the other person or culture to the specific behavior that we expect in our own culture and the deep meanings we unconsciously assume our actions have.

CAUTIONS

- **Don't** skip over this step. Take time to think and to discuss with other people as much as possible.

EXTRA CAUTION

- You are beyond the culture bump at this point!

Special instructions for groups with opposing points of view.

The primary difference between the way groups with disparate opinions actually apply the steps is whether they do the steps with one another or separately. Fundamentally, we need to be conscious of ***what*** *we say,* ***when*** *we say it and* ***with whom*** *we say it.*

Group analysis of a culture bump

If we had the action we outlined in Step Six, it would mean __________________.

Group Analysis for groups with opposing viewpoints.

Step Seven is always done separately just as Step Six was done separately. In Step Six, the two groups agreed on their specific response(s) to the issue. Now in Step Seven, the groups remain separate and begin discussions about the deeper meaning of their particular solutions. The meaning will rarely have anything to do with the original issue. This step is particularly important for working with two groups with opposing points of view as it will provide at least one possible area of commonality when the two groups come back together. As Carol states about Step Seven of her culture bump about guns on campus:

As I think about my ideas to provide a safe environment for learning, they mean hope and creativity in problem solving for me. And I don't know how this politician demonstrates hope and creativity in problem solving but I would be interested in hearing his ideas about creativity and hope.

Understanding the significance of our own expectations provides a foundation for beginning a conversation in Step Eight with the group with opposing viewpoints and allows the two sides to keep their focus on solutions rather than proving themselves right (or the others wrong).

Cautions for opposing groups

- **Do** continue to manage your emotions

- **Do** try to come up with specific details rather than generalizations
- **Don't** talk about the opposing group

21

DIVING DEEPER INTO STEP SEVEN

Diving deeper into Step Seven returns us to step five where we identified two types of commonalities that all human beings share. In that step we looked at common situations such as *responding to someone who has revealed sensitive information about themselves* In this step, we examine our assumptions about the meaning that we associate with the specific actions that we and other people do. Below is a list of opposing qualities from the Toolkit for Culture and Communication that represents just a few of the kinds of assumptions that we unconsciously associate with specific actions by ourselves and others.

1. Successful - Unsuccessful
2. Competent - Incompetent
3. Kind - Unkind
4. Modest - Show off
5. Caring - Uncaring
6. Respectful - Disrespectful
7. Considerate - Inconsiderate
8. Sensitive - Insensitive
9. Loving - Hateful
10. Comfortable - Uncomfortable
11. Helpful - Unhelpful
12. Spiritual - Unspiritual
13. "Cool" - "Dorky"
14. Decent – Indecent[51]

SECTION 8

STEP EIGHT: ASK OR THINK ABOUT HOW THOSE QUALITIES ARE DEMONSTRATED BY OTHER PEOPLE

The objective of Step Eight is to experience being connected to other people while mutually exploring individual, cultural and universal ideas.

22

STEP EIGHT: ASK OR THINK ABOUT HOW THOSE QUALITIES ARE DEMONSTRATED BY OTHER PEOPLE
(OR HOW ARE WE THE SAME?)

It seems very simple. Just have a conversation. Surely it is easy. However, Step Eight brings up three questions.

1. What is a conversation?
2. What is common ground?
3. And what does it mean to be connected?

The answers seem easy enough. If we are asked, we generally respond quickly.

- A conversation is an exchange of ideas among two or more people.
- *Simple.*
- Common ground is finding something that we agree on. *Duh*
- Being connected is having something in common. *Uh oh*

When we look at our answers to the three questions above, we discover that we are simply going in circles. But in Step Eight, we stop the cycle by stepping back and looking inside the circle.

True Conversations Versus Idle Chatter

While it is technically true that a conversation is an exchange among two or more people, the quality of a conversation varies greatly. Bernstein contrasted a true conversation with "idle chatter or a babble of competing voices."[52] Unlike babbling conversations where persons form their counter arguments as they wait for the other person to finish talking, true conversations are "an extended and open dialogue which presupposes a background of intersubjective agreements and a tacit sense of relevance." In other words, in these conversations, we agree that each person has something to say, and we further agree to actually pay attention while each person is speaking. As a result, these are conversations that can continue for a long time and while, we may not be on the same page, at least we agree that we are in the same book. Once again, we need look no farther than the internet to know that these "true conversations" are few and far between! In fact, social media demonstrates exactly how "idle chatter or a babble of competing voices" looks and sounds.

How Culture Bump Moves Past Idle Chatter

The Culture Bump Step Protocol is designed to move us beyond babbling to conversing by integrating two general approaches to differences. One approach focuses on why we are different and the second approach centers on how we are the same. In steps six and seven, we learned why we are different from other people and in Step Eight, we are ready to discover how we are the same as other people. Our commonality cannot be found in a babbling competition—we need to have a true conversation. Specifically, we need a conversation for connection. Archer has identified two types of conversations: culture-bound conversations and culture-free conversations. Culture-bound conversations rarely lead to connection but culture-free conversations always lead to connection.

All about Culture-bound Conversations

In a culture-bound conversation, participants either (1) do not acknowledge their differences at all or (2) they discuss their bumps as follows:

1. They focus is on "the other person"
2. There is little or no self-reflection
3. They learn mostly about cultural "rules" or information
4. The conversation is over and done rather quickly

Archer further points out that this kind of conversation:

> results in perpetuating and replicating the same differences in the conversation itself and in the relationship. As a consequence, the participants' bias is neither identified nor

> acknowledged and, remains firmly embedded in their unconscious, intersubjective world.[53]

In other words, it reinforces our separation from one another and, we miss the opportunity to understand ourselves as cultural beings. In short, it is a "typical" conversation without much thought, an intuitive reaction with words at another person—a conversation about why we are different. And without the Culture Bump Steps, it is a closed circle as seen in the figure below.[54]

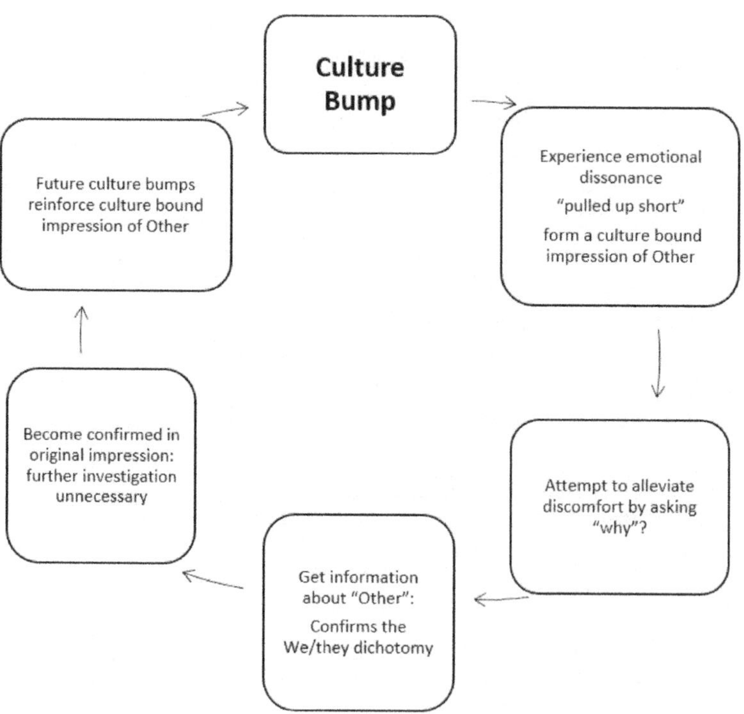

<u>All about Culture-free Conversations</u>

However, in Step Eight, we move out of this closed circle into a culture-free conversation, a conversation that results from our description of our own expectations in Step Six and our identifying the meaning for us in Step

Seven. So, we can see that culture free does not mean the absence of culture; rather it suggests that our own unconscious cultural and personal beliefs, actions and motivations have been laid bare.

In a culture-free conversation, participants (1) acknowledge their differences and (2) discuss as follows:

1. They ask how other people experience or do what they themselves experience or do
2. They share insights about themselves as individuals as well as members of a culture
3. They listen generously and speak authentically
4. The conversation is about the different ways that we are the same
5. The conversation can continue for a very long time and is one that deepens our human connection.

In these conversations, we do not change our ideas; we merely become mindful of them. We lose nothing and gain everything. In fact, we expand our life skills when we begin to understand the other person's world view—not as knowledge—but as an extension of our own horizon: we enlarge our repertoire of responses to life's situations. In other words, we learn about our actions and their actions from the perspective of a common situation that we all encounter. We just discover lots of different ways to do what we have been doing all along. As a result, we experience how everybody is the same and simultaneously, is different. Furthermore, as we and they continue to reflect on our different behavior patterns and their meanings, we all experience self-knowledge in a fusion that Richard Bernstein describes as "our own horizons being enlarged and enriched."[55] At this level of awareness, all participants are in the process of creating a shared background of commonly understood ideas. It is clear that Step Eight's culture-free conversation looks and sounds very different from a babble of competing voices, idle chatter or even polite, sincere inquiry.

The following diagram shows how the conversation can continue indefinitely.[56]

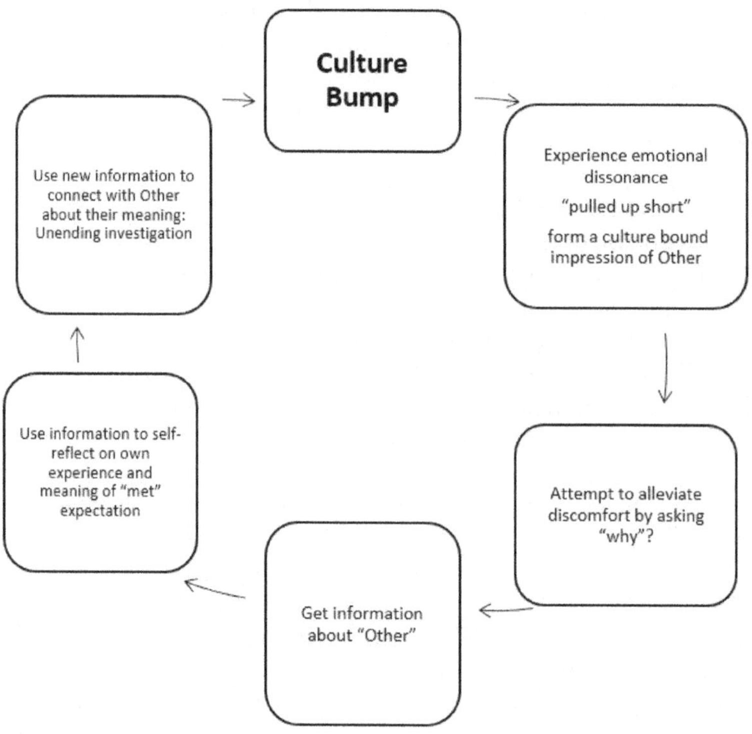

Simply put, we all know what we know and what we don't know. We have found common ground.

Understanding Common Ground and Connection

When we think of common ground, we generally understand it to be mutual understanding, and we assume that this includes agreement. While Culture Bump, culture-free conversations may include agreement, they are far more likely to consist of curiosity, surprise, new self-awareness, other-awareness and even disagreement. In short, rather than standing on solid ground, finding common ground from the Culture Bump Protocol is much more like standing on shifting sand while maintaining eye contact. All participants in a culture-free conversation are aware that the sand is shifting beneath their own and everyone else's feet, and while the sand shifts, we listen and speak and even occasionally reach out to hold one another up. In reality, what we achieve with the Culture Bump Protocol is a connection or a relationship. While a search for common ground is heartwarming, a mutually created connection is vital to sustainability.

Differences Between Connectedness and Disconnectedness

Culture Bump points out that common ground and commonalities do not imply acceptance or even agreement; they simply imply a mutually understood category in which the individuals can hold opposite points of view. Archer gives the analogy of:

> a brother and sister who disagree over the merits of vanilla ice cream versus chocolate ice cream; yet, never question their fundamental bond. Each knows where he or she stands in relation to one another.[57]

In other words, each knows that their disagreement concerns ice cream—not their sibling's sanity, humanity or right to exist (well, usually). In order to understand this, we can contrast the ideas of connectedness and disconnectedness. Archer and Nickson tied the idea of being connected or disconnected to one another to the experience of knowing how other people "see" us.

> Although the experience of disconnectedness is frequently confused with the sense of not knowing, it actually derives from a break in a primal sense of human bonding. Essentially, this sense of disconnectedness occurs because of a lack of awareness of how one's self fits into the worldview of the Other or vice versa. This is frequently accompanied by a loss of knowledge of an appropriate normative response(s) or interpretation. *(In other words, we feel disconnected when we are not sure how we are perceived by another person and, we don't know how to act with them.)*
>
> In contrast to feeling disconnected from another individual, connectedness refers to the largely unconscious state of comfort that an individual experiences when, in an interpersonal interaction, his or her expectations of the other's behavior (verbal or non-verbal responses) are known. This does not imply that the individual knows exactly how the other will respond; but rather, that the other's responses fall within a parameter of previously experienced responses. More importantly, in this state, an individual has a notion of how he or she fits into the worldview of the Other and vice versa. *(In other words, we feel*

connected to people when we know that they know that we know that they know... etc. We are in our comfort zone.)

These previously experienced responses could have been experienced directly by that particular individual or indirectly by others within that individual's culture. He or she could have learned those normative responses in many ways—for example, by observing them individually, by observing them in other people or by being formally taught. Furthermore, the individual may or may not like the responses; however, this is less important than whether or not the response which is given is within the expected cultural parameters. Even responses that are experienced as being negative are "known"—if they fall within the normative parameters. *(In other words, something can be in our comfort zone even if we don't like it; it is at least familiar.)*

Connectedness then, can be understood as the state of being that an individual experiences while in an interaction with another in which all the responses (even unpleasant responses) of all the actors are known.[58]

Possibility of Connection for All People

Clearly, by its very nature, this state of connectedness is rare with individuals who hold differing worldviews, such as liberals and conservatives in the USA or different generations or people with different national origins. All of these groups generally view one another as *us* and *them.* However, a culture-free conversation allows even these groups to experience this quality of connectedness. Habermas seems to refer to this possibility in his quote:

> World views are comparable only in respect to their potency for conferring meaning. They throw light on existential themes recurrent in every culture—birth and death, sickness and need, guilt, love, solidarity and loneliness. They open equally primordial possibilities of "making sense of human life."[59]

Archer asserts:

> Step eight assumes that a conversation about "making sense of human life" can provide the basis for forming or

> repairing a common human bond. In fact, the supposition that a culture bump initiates a break in the relationship between two people underlies all culture bump theory. Thus, when we ask one another "how" questions about existential meanings such as "guilt" or "love" or "loneliness," we instinctively fall into a culture free conversation. In this conversation, we not only understand one other but also, more importantly, repair the break in the human bond that has occurred. Ultimately, in this final step we discover that our "prejudice and ethnocentric 'blind spots' are not eliminated but are identified, acknowledged and become a part of the process itself.[60]

The objective of Step Eight is to experience being connected to the other person while mutually exploring individual, cultural and universal ideas.

23

STEPPING INTO ACTION—HAVE A CONVERSATION WITH "THEM" ABOUT HOW THEY FIND THAT MEANING

In Step Eight, you have a conversation about fundamental human qualities with another person(s).

So now you might be asking yourself, exactly how do I "work" Step Eight? How do I have a conversation with "them" about qualities or meaning. While this is perhaps the simplest step of the 8 Step Protocol, there are various parts to the step. Firstly, there is a realization that you have a blind spot about how other people experience different meanings and life-qualities. While this may feel uncomfortable initially, it generally leads to curiosity. You begin to realize that you don't know and this is your opportunity to find the answer.

Simply take the quality or qualities that you identified in Step Seven and ask the other person(s) how they express that quality. Another way to begin the conversation is to return to step Five and ask them what they might do in that universal situation.

We can understand this step better by returning to our stories:

Joy, in the first story says,

> "I realized that I have a very limited idea how Venezuelans show empathy or prefer someone to show empathy for them."

But she is now ready to have a conversation that begins with a question about empathy.

Steven and his colleagues came to realize that:

> "We're not sure how Americans feel secure or when they feel compassion or express it."

They now have conversation starter with Americans.

And Mike reports that:

> "I know that Lawrence is a considerate person, but now I'm confused about exactly how African Americans show consideration to other people in these events."

He can now begin to think more deeply or pay more attention when he is with African Americans. Having the term "culture bump" allows him to continue this conversation with his friend Lawrence.

Janice tells us,

> "I realized that Don has many ways to show he cares for me and apologizing for interrupting is not one of them."

Carol tells us that:

> "I contacted the politician quoted, and we had a conversation that lasted for several days. While we never agreed about carrying guns on campus, and in fact, he did not see the importance of creativity and hope regarding guns on campus. However, I had a number of "ah ha" moments. I clarified my own ideas and moved beyond my emotional reaction to guns on campus. In the process, I came to see Mr. Grisham in a very human light. And while I will continue to work as hard as possible to eliminate guns on campus, I would also walk across the street to introduce myself to him—should I have the opportunity. I'm pretty sure I would not have done so without the culture bump work I did above. And while he did not change his position, he ended the conversation with these words, 'Thank you for reaching out. I'm always open to respectful conversation.'"

As can be seen, the conversations frequently open more doors and more discussion. In the last example, there is a clarification—much like the brother and sister's argument about the merits of chocolate and vanilla. Carol discovered how deeply she felt and it led to doors for her to pursue, even without the politician's agreement. However, a critical difference was that her position was rooted in thoughtfulness rather than her original emotional reactionary response.

Reflect on and articulate your meaning for the behavior you identified in Step Six. Below are some sample questions to begin the conversation.

"How do you know when someone is being_________?"

"What does__________mean to you?"

"How do you express______________?"

"What are some examples of____________for you?"

"Are you________?"

"How do you feel about___________?"

More suggestions on HOW TO DO STEP EIGHT
Have a conversation with "them" about how they find that meaning

INSTRUCTIONS

1. Sometimes this conversation will trigger other insights about yourself, your community or other people. Share these insights.
2. Ask the question of other groups of people other than the ones you "bumped."
3. While this conversation begins beyond the original bump, it can circle back. However, you may have more bumps along the way. Simply repeat the steps on these new bumps.

CAUTIONS

- **Don't** skip over this step. Take time to think and discuss with as many other people as much as possible. You will notice many new ideas and insights in these conversations.
- **Don't** try to begin the conversation about the original bump. Remember this is asking about their understanding of a deeper

meaning.

- **Don't** worry if the conversation moves from your original question. The "meaning" from Step Seven is useful to begin the conversation. However, this conversation can cover many different subjects once you begin.

Special instructions for groups with opposing points of view.

The primary difference between the way groups with disparate opinions actually apply the steps is whether they do the steps with one another or separately. Fundamentally, we need to be conscious of ***what*** *we say,* ***when*** *we say it and* ***with whom*** *we say it.*

Group analysis of culture bumps

"How do you express__________?"

"What are some examples of__________for you?"

"Are you_______?"

"How do you feel about__________?"

Group Analysis for groups with opposing viewpoints.

In this eighth step, the two opposing sides come back together.

Cautions for opposing groups

- **Do** continue to manage your emotions
- **Do** take time to listen
- **Don't** rush back to the original bump too quickly. Give yourself time to really come to know the other person.

24

DIVING DEEPER INTO STEP EIGHT

Diving deeper into Step Eight reveals several concepts that are associated with this step. One of them concerns the nature of self-reflection as experienced in different cultures. Archer notes that "while some cultures allow for little reflection, other cultures include as part of their shared interpretive frame, the notion of the usefulness of self-examination. In the latter type of cultures, culture-free interactions would evolve only when an examination of their cultural notion of the usefulness of self-reflection occurs."[61] Thus, even individuals who frequently self-reflect can expect Culture Bump culture-free conversations to be a bit different.

Another way to dive deeper into understanding the on-going conversations that emerge from Step Eight is to revisit the Culture Bump Approach to culture. Because Culture Bump views culture as a collection of interpretive frames shared by groups of individuals to varying degrees along a continuum, the conversation in Step Eight can be understood as individuals discovering shared frames of reference—in which we connect—even while continuing to disagree about preferred specificities within those frames!

How does this happen? It is as though we shift our positions. Rather than "facing one another," we now figuratively sit side by side. After all, we are still different but are telling one another our different interpretations of what we both see in front of us. Archer explained that this shift emerges from the healing of our original disconnection in Steps Four through

Seven.[62]

Finally, once we familiarize ourselves with these various levels of knowledge needed in each step, we can manage our culture bumps either formally or informally. In formal acknowledgments, we reflect (using all or part of the steps) on our bump and verify our assumptions with people from the contrast culture. Informal acknowledgments occur within the context of a conversation where we immediately explore our assumptions with one another. Both types of acknowledgement provide the possibility for relieving the original, frequently unconscious feeling of anomie (or uncertainty) because they include human commonalities. Archer summarized:

> In one sense, by using the culture bump, individuals are actually carrying out personal, intercultural ethnographic research since, more than describing what happens as simple events, they are actually reconstructing the communicative rationality inherent in an interchange between individuals from differing cultures. In other words, the culture bump leads the two individuals to a place where they can become aware of their own and the other's validity claims—at an intersubjective level as well as at an objective and subjective conscious level. This correlates to step eight in the culture bump.[63]

In other words, as the character Luz Maria in Living with Strangers in the USA said, "Once we become aware of our cultural blindness, we can garner useful information about how others see themselves—rather than asking them to explain how we see them. And in order to accurately judge Others, we must use their cultural standards."[64]

SECTION 9

APPENDIX A—THE STORIES AND THEIR ANALYSIS

25

FIRST STORY: "I CAN'T BELIEVE HE SAID THAT!!"

My name is Joy from Minnesota, USA, and I had a culture bump with a nice, young man from Venezuela named Miguel. It happened like this. I had just introduced him to a friend of mine, Karen, who was another woman from the USA. She and I were in our forties while he was in his late twenties, but we were all graduate students at a university. She had mentioned that she was divorced and at one point in the conversation, had also mentioned that she was going out with several guys. He said, "So you are an international girlfriend." We all broke up laughing. I had never heard anybody say anything like that before. I could have just ignored his comment and gone on, but then I thought—hey, that caught my attention—maybe it's a culture bump. And when I actually analyzed the incident as a culture bump, I discovered some amazing things about myself and about him and Venezuelans. Now check it out!

STEP 1—Pinpoint a culture bump

"I had a culture bump with what the Venezuelan guy said to my friend and I thought it was funny."

STEP 2—Describe what he/she/it did

"Miguel said, "So you are an international girlfriend."

STEP 3—Describe what you did

"I laughed and looked at Miguel and my friend."

STEP 4—Describe your emotions when it happened.

"I felt surprised, relieved, tickled and uncertain."

STEP 5—Find the universal situation in the incident

"Responding to someone who has revealed sensitive information about themselves."

STEP 6—List your expectations for that universal situation

"When someone has revealed sensitive information about themselves, I would either joke about it or self-reveal in turn."

STEP 7—Find the meaning for you when your expectations are met

When Americans joke, it alludes to the darker side of the action while not exactly criticizing it. So, it is being critical but when I or others self-reveal in response, I think I/we are empathetic.

STEP 8—Have a conversation with "them" about how they find that meaning

"I realized that I have no idea how Venezuelans show empathy or prefer someone to show empathy for them." But I am now ready to have a conversation that begins with a question about empathy.

26

SECOND STORY: "WHAT IS THAT BIG BOX AND WHAT IS IT DOING ON MY STREET?"

My English name is Steven and I come from the People's Republic of China. I came to the USA for 6 months with a group of trainees from my company, the Chinese National Petroleum Company, to have special training at a major university. My group and I had so many culture bumps—from the moment we got off the plane! Things like putting ice in water to drink and tipping in restaurants?? But one of our biggest culture bumps happened the third day we were in the USA. It was a beautiful Saturday morning, a blue CLEAR sky (culture bump) and we three friends, Luo, Eva and I, decided to take a walk and explore our neighborhood a bit. As we came around the corner from our apartment building, we saw what looked like a small house sitting on the corner. As we got closer, we realized it wasn't a house; it didn't have a door but it had writing on it and a large scoop on the front. The word, Donations, was written on the side. We double checked the meaning of the word in our dictionary. Yep! Donations means Juankuan. We know this is a box and we know donations means Juankuan but none of this makes any sense to us. Luckily, we learned how to analyze our culture bumps in our class. Now check it out!

STEP 1—Pinpoint a culture bump

The Chinese trainees say, "We had a culture bump when we saw a donation drop box on the street and we thought it was 'weird.'"

STEP 2—Describe what he/she/it did

"We saw a wooden box (5' X 5" X5") with a tin roof and an opening in the front situated on the street that had writing on one side that said, 'Donations of clothing, shoes and toys.'"

STEP 3—Describe what you did

"Steve pointed to the box and said, 'What's that?' We all looked at the box.'"

STEP 4—Describe your emotions when it happened.

(Each one might have a different set of emotions) but one said, "We were surprised, curious and confused."

STEP 5—Find the universal situation in the incident

Helping other people who are in need

STEP 6—List your expectations for that universal situation

"When Chinese people are in need, we depend on Chinese companies and corporations to provide the bulk of charitable donations for building schools or for disasters."

STEP 7—Find the meaning for you when your expectations are met

"When we depend on Chinese companies to provide the bulk of donations for building schools or disasters, we say that we are making sure everyone is secure, we are being compassionate."

STEP 8—Have a conversation with "them" about how they find that meaning

"We're not sure how Americans feel secure or when they feel compassion or express it."

27

THIRD STORY: "WHAT IS GOING ON IN THE HOUSE OF THE LORD TODAY?"

My name is Mike and I live on a farm in Texas. A couple of months ago, my good buddy, Lawrence, invited me to go to his church for a special service on Sunday afternoon. I was looking forward to it. Oh, I am White and Lawrence is Black and I guess that's why this all came about. I got there and everybody was very nice and friendly. I felt very welcomed but maybe a bit underdressed. I noticed that most of the men were in suits and ties. I wish I had known about that. At any rate, during the service, Lawrence, stood up and walked out of the sanctuary. As he did, he raised his right arm up in the air, with his finger pointing straight up. I couldn't believe my eyes. I thought he was mad or something. I just sat there and wondered if I should get up and follow him. But in a little bit, he just came back in and sat down. Only later, did I finally ask him about it and that's when I realized it was a culture bump. I learned a lot about me and about him. Now check out my steps!

STEP 1—Pinpoint a culture bump

Mike said, "I had a culture bump when Lawrence left out of a church service in a strange way."

STEP 2—Describe what he/she/it did

"Lawrence stood up and walked out of the sanctuary while raising his right arm up in

the air, with his index finger pointing straight up."

STEP 3—Describe what you did

"I looked at him until he left the sanctuary then I looked back at the preacher."

STEP 4—Describe your emotions when it happened.

"I felt very surprised, curious, a little nervous and confused."

STEP 5—Find the universal situation in the incident

Needing to unexpectedly leave a gathering of people who are listening to a speaker.

STEP 6—List your expectations for that universal situation

"I leave out as quietly as possible, making as little eye contact as possible. If I am with someone, I might whisper, 'I'll be back shortly.'"

STEP 7—Find the meaning for you when your expectations are met

"When I leave out as quietly as possible. If I am with someone, I might whisper, 'I'll be back shortly', I think I am being considerate to the other people there at the event and the speaker."

STEP 8—Have a conversation with "them" about how they find that meaning

"I know Lawrence is a considerate person but now I'm confused about exactly how African Americans show consideration to other people in these events. I can now think more deeply or pay more attention when I am with African-Americans. Having the term "culture bump" allows me to continue this conversation with my friend, Lawrence"

28

FOURTH STORY: "GET ON WITH IT ALREADY"

My name is Janice and I have a pet peeve with my husband, Don. He interrupts me when I'm talking. It irritates me to death. It doesn't help for me to point it out to him. He just says that I tend to go on too long or sometimes, he even apologizes. But nothing seems to stop him. As I've talked about this to other women, I find a lot of my friends have a similar experience. So, I decided to do the Culture Bump Steps on this. And when I took the time to go through them, I was surprised. Now check it out!

STEP 1—Pinpoint a culture bump

"Janice said, 'I had a culture bump when I was telling my husband about my day as we were driving along when he just interrupted me to talk about a bird he saw flying along. I thought that was rude and probably happened because I am a woman.'"

STEP 2—Describe what he/she/it did

"I said, '…so then Barb texted me that she couldn't come to lunch because she was too busy. And I felt like that was pretty-.' Don said, 'Wow did you see that Mexican eagle fly over there?!'"

STEP 3—Describe what you did

"I looked at him and said, 'No.'"

STEP 4—Describe your emotions when it happened.

"I felt surprised, angry, invisible and unsure."

STEP 5—Find the universal situation in the incident

"Being excited and distracted by something when someone else is speaking."

STEP 6—List your expectations for that universal situation

"I may say, 'Wow look at that.....then say 'Sorry what were you saying?."

STEP 7—Find the meaning for you when your expectations are met

"When I say, 'Wow look at that...then say 'Sorry what were you saying?,' I think I am showing the other person I care about them."

STEP 8—Have a conversation with "them" about how they find that meaning

"I realized that Don has many ways to show he cares for me and apologizing for interrupting is not one of them."

29

FIFTH STORY: "NOT ON MY CAMPUS YOU DON'T!!!"

My name is Carol and I have taught at a university for the past twenty-five years. I've worked with lots of my culture bumps with students and folks from other countries but this was the first time I'd used the idea on something that really upset me in politics. I was reading the Sunday morning paper, drinking my coffee and reading about a guy running for office in my state. There had been a shooting (again!) on a university campus and he had been quoted as saying that we needed more guns on campus. I literally spilled my coffee! I was so upset that I threw the paper on the floor—arguing with nobody in the room. Finally, I thought that maybe I should practice what I preach in in this case. To be honest, I wasn't sure if Culture Bump would work on something like this but I sure was willing to try. Now check it out!

STEP 1—Pinpoint a culture bump

"I had a culture bump with a politician in my state about carrying guns on university campuses and I thought it was outrageous and stupid."

STEP 2—Describe what he/she/it did

"He was quoted in the newspaper as saying, 'This guy went in there and was able to kill nine people and injure about a dozen others,' said C.J. Grisham, an open carry activist who is running for state Senate. 'We won't have to worry about such a shooter going

completely unchecked until law enforcement can get there 20 minutes later. At least we'll have a chance.'"[65]

STEP 3—Describe what you did

"I read the quote."

STEP 4—Describe your emotions when it happened.

"I felt stunned, angry, fearful, sad, hopeless and despairing. I was shocked at my emotions."

STEP 5—Find the universal situation in the incident

"Ensuring a safe environment in a public place (such as a university campus)."

STEP 6—List your expectations for that universal situation

"I imagine Administrators providing a safe environment by specific actions such as: (1) having individuals sitting in classrooms or undercover campus police present at particular events and (2) Having alarm buttons on podiums as well as certain desks."

STEP 7—Find the meaning for you when your expectations are met

"I say we are being hopeful and creative in problem solving."

STEP 8—Have a conversation with "them" about how they find that meaning

"I contacted the politician quoted, and we had a conversation that lasted for several days. While we never agreed about carrying guns on campus, and in fact, he did not see the importance of creativity and hope regarding guns on campus. However, I had a number of "ah ha" moments. I clarified my own ideas and moved beyond my emotional reaction to guns on campus. In the process, I came to see Mr. Grisham in a very human light. And while I will continue to work as hard as possible to eliminate guns on campus, I would also walk across the street to introduce myself to him—should I have the opportunity. I'm pretty sure I would not have done so without the culture bump work I did above. And while he did not change his position, he ended the conversation with these words, 'Thank you for reaching out. I'm always open to respectful conversation.'"

SECTION 10

APPENDIX B—CULTURE BUMP THEORY

30

CULTURE BUMP THEORY

This chapter presents the Culture Bump Theory that has been developed over the past four decades. The Culture Bump Theory consists of a cluster of notions about the Human reaction to encountering a difference (culture bump). These include the ramifications of having a culture bump as well as a suggested protocol for responding to differences.

Definition Of A Culture Bump

However, the seminal notion in the Culture Bump Theory is the identification of, distinction of and definition of a universal phenomenon—the phenomenon of encountering something unexpected. Archer defined a culture bump as occurring when an individual from one culture finds himself or herself in a different, strange, or uncomfortable situation when interacting with persons of a different culture.[66] In the following decades, as a result of bringing this phenomenon out of our shared human intersubjective domain, a complex theory associated with the phenomenon has emerged, been examined, refined and is presented in this text. Please note that while the theory was developed using different national cultures, it applies to any type of difference—gender, ethnicity, age, region etc.

Relationship Between Culture Bumps, Perceptions And Bias

The basic theory refers to how our human response to an unexpected difference impacts our perceptions and contributes to our own personal and cultural bias. This, in turn, shapes how we view the construct of culture itself. And that construct has driven how we have attempted to ameliorate any breakdown in communication between groups, individuals or nation-states. The Culture Bump Theory, in examining these processes, has developed an alternative response.

Culture Bumps Are Pervasive And Emotional

A basic assertion in Culture Bump Theory is that culture bumps happen frequently and influence our thoughts, emotions and actions—even if we are unaware of them. Culture bumps are experienced negatively if we dislike what we encounter, positively if we like it or neutrally if we are indifferent or accustomed to what we encounter. Furthermore, the experience can change from one day to the next. This emotional aspect of "bumping" is present whether or not we are conscious of the bump. Indeed, if differences are experienced unconsciously, we simply feel vaguely disconnected or addled. If bumps are experienced consciously, we feel disconnected and perhaps distant from the Other. However, whether they are experienced consciously or unconsciously, there is a common human response.

The Innate Human Response To A Culture Bump

Archer explains that a common universal response to the discomfort or disconnection is to attempt to understand why the other person(s) acted as he or she did. This attempt emerges from an implicit assumption that if the motive were understood, the discomfort or disconnection would be alleviated. This search for motives can occur in three separate ways.

(1) We may simply explain to ourselves why we think things have occurred in a particular way—based on our own life experience.
(2) We may try to get information about the Other in some way. We may ask someone who is similar to them or get information about Others online, from an "expert" or in books.
(3) We may ask someone from our own background in an attempt to validate our own response and/or to clarify our reaction. These questions may lessen the discomfort and will garner culture-specific information about the Other. But it also confirms the initial sense of Us and Them.[67]

Why Questions Lead To Culture-Bound Interactions

The root of this separation becomes evident in the deconstruction of the Why question below:

Person with Culture Bump thinks…

- Huh? What's going on?
- Why did he/she…?
- Why doesn't he/she do what I/we do?
- Why is he/she/they different?

Archer and Nickson explain that these questions result in a particular kind of interaction termed culture-bound. They describe culture-bound interactions as follows:

> In a culture-bound interaction, participants tend to adopt coping strategies in an attempt to alleviate their feelings of anomie. Some of the characteristics of these strategies include a tendency to focus on the contrast culture, to identify the attributes of one or the other of the cultures and ultimately, to perpetuate and replicate cultural differences. The precise form that the coping strategy assumes seems to depend on the circumstances and the individual's own proclivities. One phenomenon that frequently happens is what Archer (1986) calls mirroring. Mirroring occurs when individuals from the same cultural background discuss a previously experienced culture bump. Unwittingly, they generally reinforce one another's perceptions and become confirmed in their original impression of the Other. As a consequence, their bias is neither identified nor acknowledged and remains firmly embedded in their unconscious, intersubjective world.[68]

While Archer and Nickson are referring to national culture or ethnic cultural differences, the same process applies to gender differences, religious differences, political differences or even sibling differences! Much of the interaction on social media regarding these topics are proof positive of this process. Rather than enlarging knowledge or bringing new awareness to an issue, the billions of posts reinforce bias and existing perceptions. Indeed, the more we follow our natural proclivity to learn about the Other, the more confirmed our own bias and perceptions frequently become.

Two Different Understandings Of The Definition Of Culture

A macro-cultural perspective understanding of cultural groupings of people is the result of this natural process. Archer, Kennedy, Simpson, Urquhart, and Uslu-Ok contrasted this seminal anthropological definition of culture:

> ...culture refers to the cumulative deposit of knowledge, experience, meanings, beliefs, values, attitudes, religions, concepts of self, the universe, and self-universe relationships, hierarchies of status, role expectations, spatial relations and time concepts acquired by a large

> group of people in the course of generations through individual and group striving.

With a micro-cultural perspective that is consistent with the Culture Bump Approach's definition of culture:

> Culture is viewed as a collection of interpretative frames shared by groups of individuals to varying degrees along a continuum. In this concept, the interpretative frames are never identical for any two people, and it is only when a group of individuals share a majority of similar interpretative frames that a culture can be said to exist. This definition allows for the phenomenon of individuals sharing interpretative frames with more than one group as well as for the phenomenon of individuals sharing very few interpretative frames about a particular theme. When individuals share a minimum number of interpretative frames about a particular theme, a cross-cultural relationship can be said to exist.[69]

Results Of The Traditional Understanding Of Culture

The traditional definition of culture leads to two outcomes. Firstly, individuals are viewed as products of their culture or upbringing and secondly, understanding cultural characteristics such as beliefs, values and spatial relations is considered to be the obvious way of dealing with differences. The fundamental human impulse to focus on the contrast culture, to identify the attributes of one or the other of the cultures and ultimately, to perpetuate and replicate cultural differences and the traditional definition of culture reinforce one another. And it is that definition that drove the socio-political movement in the USA from the 1950's that is outlined in Appendix C in this book.

Results Of The Culture Bump Understanding Of Culture

However, the Culture Bump Approach combines multicultural education and cross-cultural communication and steps beyond diversity. It does this by shifting the focus from "understanding cultural characteristics" as a means of dealing with differences to dealing with the difference (or the culture bump) itself. This, in turn, acknowledges the reality that people are in process with cultures or identity groups rather than being a product of a culture. Abdallah-Pretceille underscores this idea when she points out that we do not actually meet cultures; in reality, we meet an individual who is a "concentrate" of a culture expressed through their own individuality. She terms these encounters "cultural fragments" or "cultural traces." She states:

> The question of otherness arises less from a knowledge-based approach to labeling, categorization and description than from inter-subjective understanding....The singularities that are wrongly explained using the term "differences" are more directly perceptible than universality, which requires analysis. In this sense, to talk of the learning of differences is to avoid a reflection, the object of which is to bring these singularities towards a subjacent universality.[70]

Explaining The 8 Step Protocol

The Culture Bump Approach, which emerged from the theoretical understanding described earlier, has a specific protocol for consciously amplifying the instinctive process described above so as to deconstruct an encounter. This protocol embodies Abdallah-Pretceille's "reflection," and leads to an enlargement of one's worldview, a specific change mechanism and the possibility of a profound human connection with anyone.[71] The protocol consists of eight steps which are explained in-depth in the previous eight chapters.

Understanding The Knowledge Dichotomy

The first step, pinpoint a culture bump, begins the self-awareness process and simultaneously begins to develop specific skills that are necessary for successful communication with those who look, sound, act or believe differently. This conscious awareness of the specific "bump" allows the Culture Bump practitioner to restore the original break. Archer suggests that the original break is actually a knowledge dichotomy that is characterized by two phenomena that occur concurrently: a feeling of not knowing why something is happening and a subtler sense of not knowing one's role in the situation. These two fissures in the relationship can be understood as rational dissonance and emotional dissonance. The intuitive "why" response outlined above repairs the rational break while leaving the emotional rupture intact. Indeed, it seems that the emotional rupture can only be addressed by engaging in self-reflection.[72] Archer and Nickson suggest that to move beyond us and them, a Culture Bump practitioner needs to find a way to connect with the Other. They describe that state as follows:

> An unexamined culture bump frequently leads to a sense of disconnection, but a conscious examination of one's

> own culture bumps provides a sense of connection. Connectedness is the state of being that an individual experiences while in an interaction with another in which all the responses (even unpleasant responses) of all the actors are "known" within a normatively defined range that constitutes one's worldview (Archer, 1996). This largely unconscious state of comfort does not imply that the individual knows exactly how the Other will respond but, rather, that the Other's responses fall within a parameter of previously experienced responses. More importantly, in this state, an individual has a notion of how he or she fits into the worldview of the Other and vice versa. Clearly, by its very nature, this state of connectedness is rare with individuals who hold differing worldviews who generally maintain a sense of us and them. However, if they can "create" common ground, they can experience the quality of connectedness. This creation can occur through a particular type of conversation that Archer (1991) terms a culture-free conversation or interaction.[73]

How Questions Lead To Culture-Free Interactions

This culture-free conversation emerges from a second question after the intuitive why question. Using the answer to the why question, allows the Culture Bump practitioner to move into a second inquiry, How do I do THAT?

Person with Culture Bump thinks…

- How do I/we do what he/she/they SAY they are doing?
- How am I/we do what they are doing?

Specific Culture Bump Steps Develop 3 Specific Skills

While the steps guide the Culture Bump practitioner beyond the intuitive question to the ultimate step which opens an inquiry into discovering Abdallah-Preceille's "subjacent universality," they are also honing specific skill sets. Archer suggest that:

> In learning the Eight Steps, the participants are actually acquiring three fundamental skills necessary for effective cross-cultural communication: (1) the skill of detaching, (2) the skill of identifying one's own cultural positioning as being relative, and (3) the skill of finding universal meaning

> in any situation. These skills are learned as follows:
>
> Steps One, Two, Three and Four teach participants how to detach by first identifying the culture bump, giving a precise description of the difference, and finally by expressing one's emotional response to the incident. The self-reflection required in these steps results in a sense of "detachment."
>
> Steps Five and Six teach the participant how to recognize cultural relativism in oneself by identifying a universal pattern embedded in the incident and a precise description of one's expectations in the matter. The result of the self-reflection or "mirroring" with members of one's own group in these steps is a conscious awareness that one's own expectations in the incident are culturally relative.
>
> Steps Seven and Eight train the participant to look for and recognize universal meanings in any situation by requiring a determination of the meaning implicit in the fulfillment of the expectations described in Step Six. Finally, Step Eight acknowledges that there is a lack of access to the contrast culture's criteria for determining that meaning. The combination of these two steps propels the process beyond cultural relativism into an existential domain. This conscious understanding of their own epistemological workings regarding cultural differences ensures that participants emerge with confidence in their ability to communicate across cultures.[74]

Therefore, the Eight Steps guide the practitioner through a reconstructive analysis of his/her own experience of a bump.

Why The Culture Bump Steps Work

Archer and Nickson suggest that grounding for this analysis can be found in Hans Georg Gadamer's work with hermeneutics. They point out that his work offers not only a perspective for the Culture Bump Process but also a rationale for the effectiveness of the Steps.[75] Gadamer refers to a different usage in an ancient text as an "apparent absurdity" analogous to a culture bump and asserts that these absurd "bumps" can be understood only in a cyclical manner. He defines this hermeneutical cycle as first isolating a detail from the whole and then examining the whole from the perspective of the detail. The hermeneutical rule is that "It is a circular relationship in both cases…understanding that the parts, that are determined by the whole, themselves also determine this whole."[76] In turn, the Culture Bump Protocol offers a step-by-step blueprint for Gadamer's hermeneutic circle. The Culture Bump Protocol begins with pinpointing the difference (detail) then examines the universal situation implicit in the culture bump (whole). Next, describing a specific "expected" behavior returns to a (detail) and extrapolating the meaning relates to a worldview (whole). Finally, the process is reversed in a conversation with an Other beginning with their worldview.

By conflating the Culture Bump Steps with Gadamer's hermeneutical circle, the steps assure the practitioner of three outcomes:

(1) detachment,
(2) cultural relativism and
(3) universality

Specifically Steps One, Two, Three, and Four lead to detachment from the incident, Steps Five and Six reveal cultural relativism inherent in the incident and Steps Seven and Eight assure an understanding at a universal level.

Why Culture Bump Steps Lead To A Universal Connection

In addition to Gadamer's hermeneutical circle, Jurgen Habermas's theory of communicative action provides another understanding of the Culture Bump Steps. Habermas specifically validates the assumption made in the Culture Bump Theory that a universal aspect to all human discourse is possible. He speaks expressly to the universality of meaning when he says:

> World views are comparable only in respect to their potency for conferring meaning. They throw light on existential themes recurrent in every culture—birth and death, sickness and need, guilt, love, solidarity and loneliness. They open equally primordial possibilities of "making sense of human life."[77]

And the eight Culture Bump Steps, by examining—in turn—specific nuances of a personal experience, moves the Culture Bump practitioner from difference and separation to an existential awareness of one's own as well as another's world view. And in the process, both participants have a possibility of "making sense" of both of their lives.

XI

APPENDIX C—A HISTORICAL OVERVIEW OF THE CULTURE BUMP APPROACH

31

A HISTORICAL OVERVIEW OF THE CULTURE BUMP APPROACH

The Origins Of Intercultural Communication And Multicultural Studies In The USA

While cross-cultural communication has existed from the dawn of Man, its existence as a scholarly discipline is only a little over a half of a century old.[78,79,80] In the United States, Edward Hall is credited with first using the term cross-cultural communication, and the discipline of cross culture began to flourish with the 1954 case of Brown vs the Board of Education. This landmark case was the impetus to both recognize the diverse origins of American citizenry as well as provide equal opportunities for all Americans—especially those that had been systematically excluded from full participation in society. At the same time, there was an increased emphasis on developing stronger international interactions with developing countries with programs such as the Peace Corps and an influx of international students into institutions of higher education in the United States. All of these developments contributed to an increased interest in understanding differences.

Multicultural/Diversity Studies And Intercultural Communication

This heightened interest resulted in the development of two similar disciplines—multicultural education which focused on domestic issues, on issues of equity, on identifying characteristics of various minority groups and on describing how an organization would look IF all groups received equitable treatment. The second discipline was cross-cultural communication which focused on international issues, on developing specific skills for communicating effectively and on developing effective methodologies. Both disciplines contributed to bilingual education and diversity training in the business community and both focused on dealing with differences by learning about and understanding other cultural groups.

Archer points out that both multicultural studies and intercultural communication studies were concerned with changing attitudes, acquiring culture-specific information as well as developing skills.[81] Their work split into two branches—one that focused on domestic issues and one that focused on international issues.

Multicultural/Diversity Studies

The domestic branch—both multicultural education and diversity training—had a goal of fostering a better understanding of race and ethnic relations. As a result, we have a wealth of information about the various groups of people who reside in the United States. Indeed, the strength of this approach is in its identification of various groups that are not normally recognized in the countries' collective consciousness as well as in understanding the process they undergo in living in a culture in which they are not the majority. Multicultural education also underpins diversity training in both education and business in the United States.

Intercultural Communication Studies

Returning Peace Corps volunteers formed the first cadre of cross-cultural or intercultural practitioners as they grappled with the conundrum of how to train people to live and work authentically, sensitively and effectively in a foreign environment. In both the international and domestic branches, various types of training and methodologies have emerged.

Strength Of Multicultural And Intercultural Communication Studies

All of these can be seen in Hannigan's list of seventeen characteristics for effective cross-cultural communication.[82,83] Hoopes and Ventura described two types of training (1) *culture specific training* gives only information specific to a national or ethnic cultural grouping and (2) *cross-cultural training* gives conceptual information such as "perceptions," "values" and the concept of "culture" itself.[84] Fowler and Blohm and Fowler and Pusch described the methodologies that have developed through the past 50 years. These training techniques include role plays, cultural assimilators, dialogues, values clarification, and simulations as well as traditional reading and lectures.[85,86] All are based on Kolb's Model of experiential Learning that suggests that Experiential Learning occurs cyclically. First the trainee has an experience which results in an observation and a reflection which culminates in a perception which is validated. Portions of this model for cross-cultural training have been applied in business or governmental exchanges between nations as well as in domestic issues in the United States. The strength of this model has been in the development of effective cognitive and experiential methodologies.

Lack Of Change Mechanism

However, neither multicultural education and diversity training nor cross-cultural communication have a structured way to facilitate a change in the participants. Furthermore, because they focus on understanding cultural characteristics of a group of people as a means of dealing with differences, people are inevitably viewed as being a product of their culture. This perception is perpetuated by an understanding of culture as a collection of values, behaviors, beliefs and ideas to which people subscribe.

Contrasting Culture Bump Approach To Multiculturalism

In contrast, the Culture Bump Approach to differences replicates Kolb's experiential cycle by beginning with the observation of a culture bump and continuing through eight steps—each of which represents aspects of observation, self-reflection, and conceptualization. In short, the Culture Bump Approach steps beyond diversity by shifting the focus from understanding cultural characteristics as a means of dealing with differences to dealing with the difference itself. Thereby, people are viewed as being in process with culture rather than being a product of culture.

An individual's complexity is nuanced while acknowledging the influence of multiple cultures. And rather than being a static list of values and behaviors, culture is viewed as a collection of interpretative frames shared by groups of individuals to varying degrees along a continuum.[87]

The Origin And First Stage Of Culture Bump

While the Culture Bump Approach to dealing with differences is distinct from multiculturalism, it has always incorporated the advantages from cross-cultural studies. Culture Bump originated in the Fall of 1978 with the creation of a cultural component to the newly founded intensive English program, the Language & Culture Center (LCC), at the University of Houston. This component incorporated the best practices of the time, including studies from the Stanford University Institute of Intercultural Communication with its emphasis on culture-specific and cross-cultural information, studies from Dr. Pierre Cass of the World Bank as well as Archer's nascent Culture Bump Theory and Steps. As a result, the cross-cultural component of the LCC consisted of the usual elements of a traditional cross-cultural training along with the concept of culture bumps and the Culture Bump Step Protocol in addition to American culture-specific information. This foundation for culture bump development continued from 1978 to 2002 with a faculty of 2 to 5 teachers and a global student population—all contributing to Archer's original insight about Culture Bump. The ESL reader, Living with Strangers in the USA: Communicating beyond Culture, emerged from this culture-general approach with chapters and activities about perceptual differences, the cultural adjustment cycle, models for understanding cultural values, cultural communication styles, but with an additional 3 chapters on the Culture Bump Theory and Steps and a chapter on specific American cultural values.[88]

The Second Stage In Culture Bump Development

The next chapter in the development of the Culture Bump Approach occurred from 2002 to 2009 at the University of Houston Continuing Education with the development of the multi-media Toolkit for Culture and Communication. This new product reflected a shift from simply adding an explanation of the Culture Bump Theory and steps to a traditional intercultural workshop to incorporating the Culture Bump Process into each multicultural topic. Therefore, a traditional perception activity emphasizing that people have different perceptions of the same event will also focus on how to discover a shared humanity in the same event. In addition, the Toolkit incorporated two new units, not present in the earlier courses or publications, that enlarged on specific steps in the Culture Bump Protocol. These complete modules, *Emotional Intelligence* and *Human Commonalities*, are absent in traditional multicultural offerings. During its time at Continuing Education at the UH, the Culture Bump Approach was implemented in corporate training for medical facilities, global corporations and industrial plants. Ultimately, the Toolkit was available both in hard form as well as online.[89]

The Third Stage In Culture Bump Development

By 2011, when the Culture Bump Approach was housed in the Cultural Insight Program (CIP) at Auburn University, the Steps were dominant and the various multicultural concepts were enfolded into each of the steps. The Culture Bump Approach has been applied in two separate areas at

Auburn—depending on the location of the CIP. Initially, CIP was a part of the Biggio Center for the Enhancement of Teaching and Learning. As a result, Culture Bump was applied in faculty training and Train the Trainer Programs. A number of scholarly publications emanated from this chapter of the Culture Bump life. When CIP became a part of the Center for Educational Outreach & Engagement (CEOE) at Auburn University, outreach programming was developed for K-12 systems as well as continued training. An app for Culture Bump in Global Classrooms was launched in April of 2015 along with online offerings, including an upgraded online course which evolved from the original Toolkit for Communication. The insights gleaned from the use of the App contributed to the completion of the present Culture Bump Step-centric Approach for dealing with differences found in this text. In this approach, the Culture Bump Steps are the framework for an intercultural training with multicultural units such as perceptions or cultural values feeding into each step as needed rather than as standalone units.

XI

APPENDIX D— CULTURE BUMP PROTOCOL FORMS

These forms are for practicing your own culture bumps.

Step 1: Pinpoint the culture bump

I had a culture bump with_____________and I thought that was______________.

Step 2: Describe what the other person(s) did

What did the other person(s) do?_____________________________________

OR *in the case of an object, describe it physically.*

Step 3: Describe what you did

What did I do or say? I____.

Step 4: List the emotions you felt when the bump happened.

At the time of the bump, the emotions I felt were:_____________________.

Step 5: Find the universal situation in the culture bump

Why did the other person(s) do what they did?__________________________.

Step 6: Describe what you would do or would expect other(s) to do in that situation.

Describe at least one of your expected behaviors in that situation. I expect____.

Step 7: Find the meaning for you when your expectations are met

When people in my culture or my group, do (Step Six's answer)_______________,
I say they are ____.

Step 8: Have a conversation about how others find that same meaning.

How do you/they know when someone is being_______________________?
What does_______________________mean to you?
How do you express_______________________?
What are some examples of _______________________for you?
Is_______________________important to you?

Step 1: Pinpoint the culture bump

I had a culture bump with_____________and I thought that was______________.

Step 2: Describe what the other person(s) did

What did the other person(s) do?_______________________________________

OR *in the case of an object, describe it physically.*

Step 3: Describe what you did

What did I do or say? I____.

Step 4: List the emotions you felt when the bump happened.

At the time of the bump, the emotions I felt were:_______________________.

Step 5: Find the universal situation in the culture bump

Why did the other person(s) do what they did?_____________________________.

Step 6: Describe what you would do or would expect other(s) to do in that situation.

Describe at least one of your expected behaviors in that situation. I expect____.

Step 7: Find the meaning for you when your expectations are met

When people in my culture or my group, do (Step Six's answer)____________________,
I say they are ____.

Step 8: Have a conversation about how others find that same meaning.

How do you/they know when someone is being___________________________?
What does___________________________mean to you?
How do you express___________________________?
What are some examples of ___________________________for you?
Is___________________________important to you?

Step 1: Pinpoint the culture bump

I had a culture bump with______________and I thought that was_______________.

Step 2: Describe what the other person(s) did

What did the other person(s) do?______________________________________

OR *in the case of an object, describe it physically.*

Step 3: Describe what you did

What did I do or say? I____.

Step 4: List the emotions you felt when the bump happened.

At the time of the bump, the emotions I felt were:_______________________.

Step 5: Find the universal situation in the culture bump

Why did the other person(s) do what they did?____________________________.

Step 6: Describe what you would do or would expect other(s) to do in that situation.

Describe at least one of your expected behaviors in that situation. I expect____.

Step 7: Find the meaning for you when your expectations are met

When people in my culture or my group, do (Step Six's answer)______________________,
I say they are ____.

Step 8: Have a conversation about how others find that same meaning.

How do you/ they know when someone is being__________________________?
What does___________________________mean to you?
How do you express__________________________?
What are some examples of__________________________for you?
Is____________________________important to you?

WORKS CITED

1 Archer, C. M. (1986). Culture Bump and Beyond. In *Culture Bound: Bridging the Cultural Gap in Language Teaching.* Cambridge: Cambridge University Press.

2 Archer, C. M. (1991). *Living with strangers in the U.S.A.: Communicating Beyond Culture.* New York, NY: Prentice Hall.

3 Archer, C. M. (1986). Culture Bump and Beyond. In *Culture Bound: Bridging the Cultural Gap in Language Teaching.* Cambridge: Cambridge University Press.

4 Leppihalme, R. (1997). Culture Bumps: An Empirical Approach to the Translation of Allusions. *Multilingual Matter.*

5 Archer, C. M. (1986). Culture Bump and Beyond. In *Culture Bound: Bridging the Cultural Gap in Language Teaching.* Cambridge: Cambridge University Press.

6 Jiang, W. (2001). Handling "Culture Bumps". *ELT Journal,55*(4), 382-390.

7 Holmes, S. Y., & Simpson, J. S. (2012, January). *Stop at the Culture Bump: Assisting Educators in Acknowledging Their Cultural Identity.* Lecture presented at Association for Science Teacher Education in FL, Clearwater.

8 Seelye, H. N. (1984). *Teaching culture strategies for intercultural communication.* Lincolnwood, IL: National Textbook Comp.

9 Archer, C. M., & Nickson, S. C. (2012). The Role of Culture Bump in Developing Intercultural Communication Competency and Internationalizing Psychology Education. *Psychology Learning & Teaching,11*(3), 335-343.

10 Nickson, S. C., Archer, C. M., & Chaudhury, S. R. (2013). The Impact of Culture Bump and Technology on Creating Effective Diversity Leadership. *IGI Global,* 147-155.

STEP ONE: PINPOINT THE CULTURE BUMP (OR NAME IT AND CLAIM IT)

11 Archer, C. M. (1986). Culture Bump and Beyond. In *Culture Bound: Bridging the Cultural Gap in Language Teaching*. Cambridge: Cambridge University Press.

12 Archer, C. M., & Nickson, S. C. (2012). The Role of Culture Bump in Developing Intercultural Communication Competency and Internationalizing Psychology Education. *Psychology Learning & Teaching,11*(3), 335-343.

13 Abdallah-Pretceille, M. (2006). Interculturalism as a paradigm for thinking about diversity. *Intercultural Education,17* (5), 475-483.

14 Shaules, J. (2019). Edward Hall Ahead of his time: Deep culture, intercultural understanding and embodied cognition. *Intercultural Communication Education*, 2(1), 1-19.

15 Hall, E. T. (1959). *The Silent Language*. Garden City, NY: Anchor Press.

16 Archer, C. M., & Nickson, S. C. (2012). The Role of Culture Bump in Developing Intercultural Communication Competency and Internationalizing Psychology Education. *Psychology Learning & Teaching,11*(3), 335-343.

STEPPING INTO ACTION—PINPOINT THE CULTURE BUMP

17 Wemund, B. (2015, October 2). Oregon Shooting Comes as Texas Schools Grapple with Guns on Campus. *Houston Chronicle.*

DIVING DEEPER INTO STEP ONE

18 Archer, C. M. (1991) *Living with Strangers in the U.S.A.: Communicating Beyond Culture.* New York, NY: Prentice Hall.

STEP TWO: DESCRIBE WHAT S/HE/THEY DID (OR JUST THE FACTS, MA'AM)

19 Archer, C. M., & Nickson, S. C. (2012). The Role of Culture Bump in Developing Intercultural Communication Competency and Internationalizing Psychology Education. *Psychology Learning & Teaching,11*(3), 407.

20 Carspecken, P. F. (1996). *Critical Ethnography in Educational Research A Theoretical and Practical Guide.* New York: Routledge and Kegan Paul Limited.

21 Archer, C. M. (1996). *A Qualitative Study of the Communicative Experience of a Venezuelan and a North American* (Unpublished doctoral dissertation). University of Houston.

STEPPING INTO ACTION—DESCRIBE WHAT HE/SHE/THEY

DID

22 Wemund, B. (2015, October 2). Oregon Shooting Comes as Texas Schools Grapple with Guns on Campus. *Houston Chronicle.*

DIVING DEEPER INTO STEP TWO

23 Archer, C. M. (2004) *Toolkit for Culture & Communication.* Houston, TX: University of Houston

DIVING DEEPER INTO STEP THREE

24 Archer, C. M. (1996) A Qualitative Study of the Communicative Experience of a Venezuelan and a North American (Unpublished doctoral dissertation). University of Houston, 152.

STEP FOUR: LIST YOUR EMOTIONS WHEN IT HAPPENED (OR BRINGING IT

25 Archer, C. M (2004) Toolkit for Culture & Communication. Published by University of Houston. p. 63)

26 Goleman, D. (1995). *Emotional Intelligence.* New York, NY: Bantam Books.

27 Archer, C. M., & Nickson, S. C. (2012). The Role of Culture Bump in Developing Intercultural Communication Competency and Internationalizing Psychology Education. *Psychology Learning & Teaching, 11*(3), *421.*

28 Archer, C. M. (1996). *A Qualitative Study of the Communicative Experience of a Venezuelan and a North American* (Unpublished doctoral dissertation). University of Houston.

29 Archer, C. M., & Nickson, S. C. (2012). The Role of Culture Bump in Developing Intercultural Communication Competency and Internationalizing Psychology Education. *Psychology Learning & Teaching, 11*(3), 335.

DIVING DEEPER INTO STEP FOUR

30 Goleman, D. (1995) *Emotional Intelligence.* New York, NY: Bantam, 63-64

STEP FIVE: FIND THE UNIVERSAL SITUATION IN THE INCIDENT (OR STEPPING OUTSIDE)

31 Archer, C. M., Dr. (2004). *Toolkit for Culture & Communication.* Houston, TX: University of Houston.

32 Archer, C. M., Kennedy, B., Simpson, M., Urquhart, G., & Uslu-Ok, D. (2015). Cultural Differences in the Classroom? There's an app for that! *Journal of Assessment and Teaching of English Language Learners, 1.*

33 Abdallah-Pretceille, M. (2006). Interculturalism as a paradigm for

thinking about diversity. *Intercultural Education, 17* (5), 476-477.
34 Archer, C. M. (1996). *A qualitative study of the communicative experience of a Venezuelan and a North American*(Unpublished doctoral dissertation). University of Houston. 25-26.

DIVING DEEPER INTO STEP FIVE

35 Archer, C. M. (2004) *Toolkit for Culture & Communication.* Houston, TX: University of Houston

STEP SIX: LIST YOUR EXPECTATIONS FOR THAT UNIVERSAL (OR NORMAL IS JUST A SETTING ON A WASHING MACHINE)

36 Archer, C. M. (1996). *A Qualitative Study of the Communicative Experience of a Venezuelan and a North American* (Unpublished doctoral dissertation). University of Houston.
37 Hall, E. T. (1959). *The Silent Language.* Garden City, NY: Anchor Press.
38 Bernstein, R. J. (1983). *Beyond Objectivism and Relativism: Science, Hermeneutics, and Praxis.* Philadelphia: Univ. of Pennsylvania Press. 202.
39 Habermas, J. (1984). *The Theory of Communicative Action: Reason and the Rationalization of Society* (Vol. 1). Boston, MA: Beacon Press.
40 Archer, C. M. (1996). *A Qualitative Study of the Communicative Experience of a Venezuelan and a North American* (Unpublished doctoral dissertation). University of Houston.
41 Archer, C. M. (1986). Culture Bump and Beyond. In *Culture Bound: Bridging the Cultural Gap in Language Teaching.* Cambridge: Cambridge University Press.
42 Archer, C. M. (1991). *Living with strangers in the U.S.A.: Communicating Beyond Culture.* New York, NY: Prentice Hall.
43 Archer, C. M., Kennedy, B., Simpson, M., Urquhart, G., & Uslu-Ok, D. (2015). Cultural Differences in the Classroom? There's an app for that! *Journal of Assessment and Teaching of English Language Learners, 1.*
44 Gadamer, H. (1975). *Truth and Method.* London: Sheed and Ward.
45 Archer, C. M. (1996). *A Qualitative Study of the Communicative Experience of a Venezuelan and a North American* (Unpublished doctoral dissertation). University of Houston. 173.
46 Archer, C. M., & Nickson, S. C. (2012). The Role of Culture Bump in Developing Intercultural Communication Competency and Internationalizing Psychology Education. *Psychology Learning & Teaching, 11*(3), *340.*
47 Archer, C. M., & Nickson, S. C. (2012). The Role of Culture Bump in Developing Intercultural Communication Competency and

Internationalizing Psychology Education. *Psychology Learning & Teaching, 11*(3), 336.

DIVING DEEPER INTO STEP SIX

48 Pierre Cass (1980) *Training for the Cross-Cultural Mind: A Handbook for Cross Cultural Trainers and Consultants.* Society for Intercultural Education, Training and Research, Washington, D. C., 1980, p. 48

STEP SEVEN: FIND THE MEANING FOR YOU WHEN YOUR EXPECTATIONS ARE MET (OR WHY, OH WHY, DO WE DO WHAT WE DO?)

49 Archer, C. M. (1996). *A qualitative study of the communicative experience of a Venezuelan and a North American*(Unpublished doctoral dissertation). University of Houston.

50 Archer, C. M. (1991). *Living with strangers in the U.S.A.: Communicating Beyond Culture.* New York, NY: Prentice Hall.

DIVING DEEPER INTO STEP SEVEN

51 Archer, C. M. (2004) *Toolkit for Culture & Communication.* Houston, TX: University of Houston

STEP EIGHT: HAVE A CONVERSATION WITH "THEM" ABOUT HOW THEY FIND THAT MEANING (OR HOW ARE WE THE SAME?)

52 Bernstein, R. J. (1983). *Beyond Objectivism and Relativism: Science, Hermeneutics, and Praxis.* Philadelphia: Univ. of Pennsylvania Press. 2

53 Archer, C. M. (1996). *A Qualitative Study of the Communicative Experience of a Venezuelan and a North American* (Unpublished doctoral dissertation). University of Houston. 175.

54 Archer, C. M., & Nickson, S. C. (2012). The Role of Culture Bump in Developing Intercultural Communication Competency and Internationalizing Psychology Education. *Psychology Learning & Teaching, 11*(3), 410.

55 Bernstein, R. J. (1983). *Beyond Objectivism and Relativism: Science, Hermeneutics, and Praxis.* Philadelphia: Univ. of Pennsylvania Press. 143

56 Archer, C. M., & Nickson, S. C. (2012). The Role of Culture Bump in Developing Intercultural Communication Competency and Internationalizing Psychology Education. *Psychology Learning & Teaching, 11*(3), 412.

57 Archer, C. M. (1996). *A Qualitative Study of the Communicative Experience of a Venezuelan and a North American* (Unpublished doctoral

dissertation). University of Houston.

58 Archer, C. M., & Nickson, S. C. (2012). The Role of Culture Bump in Developing Intercultural Communication Competency and Internationalizing Psychology Education. *Psychology Learning & Teaching, 11*(3)

59 Habermas, J. (1984). *The Theory of Communicative Action: Reason and the Rationalization of Society* (Vol. 1). Boston, MA: Beacon Press. 59.

60 Archer, C. M. (1996). *A Qualitative Study of the Communicative Experience of a Venezuelan and a North American* (Unpublished doctoral dissertation). University of Houston.

DIVING DEEPER INTO STEP EIGHT

61 Archer, C. M. (1996). *A Qualitative Study of the Communicative Experience of a Venezuelan and a North American* (Unpublished doctoral dissertation). University of Houston.

62 Archer, C. M. (1996). *A Qualitative Study of the Communicative Experience of a Venezuelan and a North American* (Unpublished doctoral dissertation). University of Houston.

63 Archer, C. M. (1996). *A Qualitative Study of the Communicative Experience of a Venezuelan and a North American* (Unpublished doctoral dissertation). University of Houston.

64 Archer, C. M. (1991). *Living with strangers in the U.S.A.: Communicating Beyond Culture.* New York, NY: Prentice Hall.

FIFTH STORY: "NOT ON MY CAMPUS YOU DON'T!!!"

65 Wemund, B. (2015, October 2). Oregon Shooting Comes as Texas Schools Grapple with Guns on Campus. *Houston Chronicle.*

CULTURE BUMP THEORY

66 Archer, C. M. (1986). Culture Bump and Beyond. In *Culture Bound: Bridging the Cultural Gap in Language Teaching.* Cambridge: Cambridge University Press.

67 Archer, C. M. (1996). *A Qualitative Study of the Communicative Experience of a Venezuelan and a North American* (Unpublished doctoral dissertation). University of Houston.

68 Archer, C. M., & Nickson, S. C. (2012). The Role of Culture Bump in Developing Intercultural Communication Competency and Internationalizing Psychology Education. *Psychology Learning & Teaching, 11*(3),

69 Archer, C. M., Kennedy, B., Simpson, M., Urquhart, G., & Uslu-Ok, D. (2015). Cultural Differences in the Classroom? There's an app for that! *Journal of Assessment and Teaching of English Language Learners, 1.*

70 Abdallah-Pretceille, M. (2006). Interculturalism as a paradigm for thinking about diversity. *Intercultural Education,17* (5), 475-483.

71 Abdallah-Pretceille, M. (2006). Interculturalism as a paradigm for thinking about diversity. *Intercultural Education,17* (5), 475-483.

72 Archer, C. M. (1996). *A Qualitative Study of the Communicative Experience of a Venezuelan and a North American* (Unpublished doctoral dissertation). University of Houston.

73 Archer, C. M., & Nickson, S. C. (2012). The Role of Culture Bump in Developing Intercultural Communication Competency and Internationalizing Psychology Education. *Psychology Learning & Teaching, 11*(3).

74 Archer, C. M., & Nickson, S. C. (2012). The Role of Culture Bump in Developing Intercultural Communication Competency and Internationalizing Psychology Education. *Psychology Learning & Teaching, 11*(3), *421*

75 Archer, C. M., & Nickson, S. C. (2012). The Role of Culture Bump in Developing Intercultural Communication Competency and Internationalizing Psychology Education. *Psychology Learning & Teaching, 11*(3)

76 Gadamer, H. (1975). *Truth and Method.* London: Sheed and Ward. 258-259.

77 Habermas, J. (1984). *The Theory of Communicative Action: Reason and the Rationalization of Society* (Vol. 1). Boston, MA: Beacon Press. *59*

A HISTORICAL OVERVIEW OF THE CULTURE BUMP APPROACH

78 Archer, C. (2011, December 19). Training for effective cross cultural communication. Retrieved from https://culturebump.com/articles/training-for-effectivecross-cultural-communication/

79 Samover, L., & Porter, R. (1976). *Intercultural Communication: A Reader* (2nd ed.). Belmont, CA: Wadsworth Publishing Company

80 Aneas, M. A., & Sandin, M. P. (2009). Intercultural and Cross-Cultural Communication Research: Some Reflections about Culture and Qualitative Methods. *Forum Qualitative Social Research, 10* (1).

81 Nickson, S. C., Archer, C. M., & Chaudhury, S. R. (2013). The Impact of Culture Bump and Technology on Creating Effective Diversity Leadership. *IGI Global,* 147-155.

82 Hannigan, T. P. (1990). Traits, Attitudes, and Skills that are Related to Intercultural Effectiveness and Their Implications for Cross-cultural Training: A Review of the Literature. *International Journal of Intercultural Relations, 14*(1), 89-111.

83 Kohls, L. R. (1979). *Survival kit for overseas living.* Chicago, IL: Intercultural Press.

84 Hoopes, D. S., & Ventura, P. (n.d.). *Intercultural sourcebook.* Yarmouth, Me: Intercultural Press.

85 Fowler, S. M., & Blohm, J. M. (n.d.). An Analysis of Methods for Intercultural Training. In *Handbook of Intercultural Training*(pp. 37-84). Thousand Oaks, CA: Sage Publications.

86 Fowler, S. M., & Pusch, M. D. (2010). Intercultural Simulation Games: A Review (of the United States and Beyond). *Simulation & Gaming, 41*(1), 94-115.

87 Archer, C. M. (1996). *A Qualitative Study of the Communicative Experience of a Venezuelan and a North American* (Unpublished doctoral dissertation). University of Houston. 151.

88 Archer, C. M. (1991). *Living with strangers in the U.S.A.: Communicating Beyond Culture.* New York, NY: Prentice Hall.

89 Archer, C. M. (2004). *Toolkit for Culture & Communication.* Houston, TX: University of Houston. 144.

90 Archer, C. M., Kennedy, B., Simpson, M., Urquhart, G., & Uslu-Ok, D. (2015). Cultural Differences in the Classroom? There's an app for that! *Journal of Assessment and Teaching of English Language Learners, 1.* 145.

(left: Dr. Carol Archer, right: Dr. Stacey Nickson)

ABOUT THE AUTHORS

Dr. Carol Archer

Dr. Carol Archer is the originator of the Culture Bump Approach and methodology. She first started working with the Culture Bump Approach in October of 1978 at the University of Houston and has since trained people in various fields, such as international business, religion, education, and medicine, to use the approach in their work and lives. In addition to researching the Culture Bump Approach and using it in classroom settings, she has worked with companies like AT&T, Pecten/Shell Oil, Exxon and the World Trade Association to train over 1,000 businessmen and women from the Middle East, Asia, Latin America, and the USA using the Culture Bump Approach. She is the author and creator of the Culture Bump products, *Living with Strangers in the U.S.A: Communicating Beyond Culture*, and the *Toolkit for Culture and Communication.*

Dr. Stacey Nickson

Culture Bump began partnering with Auburn University in 2012 under the guidance of Dr. Stacey Nickson, Director of Auburn's Center for Educational Outreach & Engagement. She created and administers the Auburn University Cultural Insight Program as a home for research, training and product development using the Culture Bump Approach. As such, she presents workshops and seminars locally, nationally and internationally to train educational leaders from varied disciplines in cross-cultural communication. She is on the National Fulbright Association Board of Directors and is former President of the Alabama Fulbright Association.

Made in the USA
Columbia, SC
15 March 2021

34308263R00078